B

Vir

Brief Lives:
Virginia Woolf

E.H. Wright

Brief Lives
Published by Hesperus Press Limited
19 Bulstrode Street, London w1u 2jn
www.hesperuspress.com

First published by Hesperus Press Limited, 2011

Designed and typeset by Fraser Muggeridge studio
Printed by CPI Group (UK) Ltd, Croydon cr0 4yy

isbn: 978-1-84391-909-4

Contents

Introduction – Reading, Writing and Life

'My God, how does one write a Biography? Tell me.
[...] How can one deal with facts – so many and so many
and so many? Or ought one, as I incline, to be purely
fictitious. And what is a life?'

– *The Letters of Virginia Woolf*

In 1885, Sir Leslie Stephen became one of the founding editors of
the *Dictionary of National Biography*; his second daughter, Adeline
Virginia, by his second wife, Julia Princep, was only three years
old – it was a significant context in which to be born. The
Dictionary of National Biography helped to ignite Virginia's interest in life writing, though she despised the amount of pressure
it put upon her father. This flame was fanned by the Victorian
penchant for the biographies of great men, many of which he
encouraged her to read. Indeed, Virginia had read works such as
Froude's *Life of Carlyle*, Lockhart's *Memoirs of the Life of Sir Walter
Scott*, and *Essays in Ecclesiastical Biography* by her grandfather
James Stephen among many others before the age of fifteen.
However, she soon began to reflect that these authors had failed
to catch the real person beneath the social façade and that
women were noticeably lacking as the subjects of biography.
Indeed, the traditional biographies, often written by surviving
family members, deliberately tried to obscure the truth for fear
of denigrating the memory of their subject (a problem she

would encounter herself when she came to write the biography of her friend Roger Fry in the 1930s). The 'problem of biography', as Virginia reflected in her essay 'The New Biography' (1927), was to combine the 'granite-like solidity' of truth with the 'rainbow-like intangibility' of personality. It remains a problem for biographers today including the many who have attempted to write the life of the now legendary Virginia Woolf – a writer whose reputation precedes her and often sadly distorts readings of her fiction. A mad woman, a snob, a feminist, a recluse, a socialite, a genius, many of these terms are contradictory and Virginia has been represented as all of them, but these epithets, though true in part, suit only specific moments in her life and are individual facets of her complex character. While gathering recollections of her from those who knew her personally, Joan Russell Noble was told that

> to describe her was as difficult as 'trying to count the colours in a floating bubble: it vanished before you had time to begin'; her nature was so complex and so varied that it could only be glimpsed from time to time, and then never seen as a whole. For some who said they would try to write about her – though by no means for all – it produced a kind of mental agony, almost a mental block. The more intimately one had known her, it seemed, the harder it was to say exactly what was true about her.[1]

Therefore, though the facts of her life are relatively simple to set down, this biography, as with any attempt to write out a life, can only hint at what Virginia Woolf as a person was really like.

Luckily for biographers of Virginia Woolf she left, not only a collection of memoir papers, but several diary notebooks and thousands of letters, all of which make her worthy of being called one of the greatest literary epistolarians and diarists of the twentieth century. The memoir papers are collected into a single volume published as *Moments of Being*, while the letters and diaries are collected and published in twelve volumes. In their introduction to Volume One of Virginia's letters, Nigel Nicolson and Joanne Trautmann note that 'she wrote as she talked, brilliantly' and it is clear from responses to her letters that they were treasured and applauded by the recipients. Virginia's sister, the painter Vanessa Bell (*née* Stephen), often related the delight with which they were received by her extended family: 'It was very difficult not to read aloud bits of your letters and it seemed as harmless as anything could well be – Clive simply raved about your brilliance and we discussed your gifts as a letter writer compared to Mrs Carlyle.' And later: 'The family was enraptured by your last letter. If only, Angelica [Virginia's niece] said, it could go on forever – I had to read it all aloud twice over.'[2]

Though not primarily designed for performance, Virginia's letters were often read aloud for the amusement of others. Although Virginia denied this sense of audience and preferred her letters to be kept only for the addressee, Vanessa accused her sister of having a 'true literary mind [which] does not feel any sympathy'[3] for this sense of privacy. In an early letter to her husband Clive Bell, Vanessa noticed that her sister's letters gained by this awareness of a larger readership than just the addressee: 'I think the Goat's [Virginia's] letters are distinctly more amusing when she imagines you to be one of her audience'.[4] The earliest of Virginia's letters, a collaboration with her father when she was only six years old, was written to her 'sponsor', James Russell Lowell, telling him he is 'a naughty man not to come here', and the last is a suicide note to her husband Leonard Woolf in March 1941. Of course only a fraction of her letters survive, dependent as they were on the good will and fastidiousness of recipients in keeping them; for example, though she states on 7th August 1908 that she 'must now write to Nelly, Violet, Dorothea, Nun, Aunt Mary and […] should write to Olive', the editors point out that only this letter to Vanessa survives.

Virginia wrote letters for a variety of reasons. They were primarily a way to keep in intimate contact with family and friends, from whom she demanded news, affection, praise and opinions. 'A true letter, so my theory runs,' she wrote to Clive Bell, 'should be as a film of wax pressed close to the graving of the mind', though she admits that in following her 'own prescription this sheet would be scored with some very tortuous and angular incisions'. They also gave her the opportunity to write off her criticism of people, places and events; criticism that could often be quite hilarious, as well as extremely scathing, such as her descriptions of Lady Ottoline Morrell whom she characterised as an ugly Medusa. 'That mustn't be repeated,' she would remind herself, knowing full well that this is exactly what she was likely to do. She asked her friend Violet Dickinson to burn her letters and told Ottoline that she would stop confiding anything to her should she allow others to read them; such claims were at odds with her sister's opinions on Virginia's letters as performance pieces. Though she claimed to '*hate* and *detest* writing letters' and in a letter to Duncan Grant crudely likened writing them to defecating, she loved to receive them, often begging the recipient to write back as soon as possible. Letters were a chance to gather information, ideas and inspiration for her fiction, as well as being an opportunity to practise her writing style and to try out alternative personae.

However, Virginia's diaries offer an even more personal view of her thoughts and feelings about her life and art. Luckily for the Virginia Woolf scholar she did not adhere to her resolution in September 1897 to 'fling diaries & diarising into the corner – to dust & mice & moths & all creeping crawling eating destroying creatures'. Uncensored by the consciousness of a reader, they are unguarded, alternately amusing and angry, reflective and melancholy; they, more than her letters, gave Virginia the opportunity to test her creative powers and writing style before attempting them more formally in her fiction. They also show how closely her art and her life were moulded together, as many of the characters and events she writes about in her diaries find their way into her fiction, though often embellished or transmuted 'as in a fairground mirror'.[5] She understood that the speed and care-lessness with which her diary was written was also its greatest strength in terms of using it for future inspiration: 'if I stopped and took thought, it would never be written at all; & the advant-age of the method is that it sweeps up accidentally several stray matters which I should exclude if I hesitated, but which are the diamonds of the dustheap.' She characterized it as 'some deep old desk, or capacious hold-all, in which one flings a mass of odds and ends without looking them through'; and she must not, she reminds herself, 'play the part of the censor'. The diary helped her to 'loosen' her writing 'ligaments'. 'I believe,' she reflected, 'that during the past year I can trace some increase of ease in my professional writing which I attribute to my casual half hours [of diary writing] after tea.' Her diaries also provided her with a store to plunder for her own memoirs which she eventually began to write a year before her suicide. As early as January 1919 she noted to the future self who would write these memoirs: 'But how I envy her the task I am preparing for her! There is none I should like better.'

In addition to her fame as a diarist, Virginia Woolf is noted for being one of the most well-read people of her generation. She claimed to her brother Thoby in July 1901: 'I want to read myself blue in the nose' and recalled in her memoir 'A Sketch of the Past' how she would 'read [her]self into a trance of perfect bliss'. Her reading lists were impressive – fiction, drama, poetry, biography, history, science, philosophy – everything was of inter-est. Books were an escape from the everyday, they gave her 'great fun & pleasure', but they were also a very important part of her creative process. 'Reading makes me intensely happy, and culminates in a fit of writing always,' she wrote to Violet Dickinson in January 1905. Though reading was clearly inspira-tional for her creativity, writing was not always as easy or instan-taneous. Virginia reflected at the beginning of her career that when she tried to write about a subject the words would often fail to come, but that in 'one month, or three or seven, suddenly without any bidding, [the brain] pours out the whole picture, gratuitously.' She wrote her novels carefully, often redrafting sentences, sections or the whole book several times before submitting them to other eyes. Her perfectionism could make writing a painful process, and a pattern of illness emerged as she became unwell, sometimes seriously, after each novel. Her project to revolutionise fiction was brave and adventurous, as was the partnership she formed to run the Hogarth Press with her husband.

However, difficult and arduous as writing was to Virginia, it was not an activity she could live without – writing and life were inextricably linked. In a draft memoir begun in 1940, Virginia described writing as 'the good friend who is with me still', and noted that she retained throughout her life the 'sense of the spectacle; the dispassionate separate sense that [she was] seeing what will be useful later' and that she 'could even find the words for the scene as [she] stood there'. Life was the ultimate inspiration for her work, though she was clear that it was not directly translated into her fiction. She disliked, for example, being told by Herbert Fisher in his autobiography that the characters in her novels were her friends and relations, 'when' as she pointed out, 'being in a novel, they're not'.

Though a writer of one serious and two mock biographies and numerous smaller biographical sketches, and despite having 'a passion for biographies', Virginia disliked the idea that her own life would be written about. She despised the studies of her novels that came out during her lifetime; she was sensitive to criticism; and was uncomfortable with any unwanted invasions of her privacy. 'I feel always that writing is a reticent thing to be kept in the dark – like hysterics,' she claimed to Lady Robert Cecil. Her books, lectures, broadcasts and journalism were for the public domain, but her life, contained in the diaries, letters, unfinished memoirs and drafts of her novels, was private and writing about it prohibited. She forbade her future self 'to let the eye of man behold [her diary]' and reminded the older Virginia 'of the existence of the fireplace, where she has my leave to burn these pages to so many black films with red eyes in them'. In her last letter to Leonard before her suicide on 28th March 1941, she ordered him to 'burn all my papers' – luckily for us he did not. Her diaries and letters reveal her process in detail, while the drafts and redrafts of her novels, shorter fiction and articles tell the story of an author devoted to her art. The existence of Virginia Woolf's private writings, as well as her published works, have been invaluable to this biography, which gives Virginia's 'common reader' a brief insight into the life and work of one of the seminal British Modernist writers.

A Note on the Text

Please note that Virginia Woolf's idiosyncratic spelling and punctuation, and her use of the ampersand, have been retained in the quotations taken from the published volumes of her diaries and letters.

22 Hyde Park Gate

'Consciously but truly impressive, old, solitary and deserted,' thus Virginia Stephen recalled her father three years after his death in 'Reminiscences', a memoir addressed to her sister's first child. Sir Leslie Stephen was a difficult figure for his children to like and at times to respect, though he was one of the most influential figures in their Victorian London childhood and adolescence. He was fifty when Virginia was born and represented to his youngest children a different era which venerated the British Empire, believed in the class system and governed the complex and trap-strewn codes of Victorian social etiquette. Virginia blamed her uncomfortable adolescence on the fact that her father was 'living in 1860' while 'we [his four youngest children] were living say in 1910.'

Born on 28th November 1832, to James and Jane Stephen (*née* Venn), Leslie had, as Virginia put it, 'one foot in Clapham, the other in Downing Street. Such is the obvious first sentence of his biography.' He came from a long line of professionals: lawyers, lecturers, colonial servants and politicians, but his outlook was augmented by links to the Quaker Clapham Sect whose social conscience, work ethic and intellectual agility he inherited and passed on to his children. He also passed on a family tendency to mental and emotional breakdowns, which he called 'the fidgets' and 'fits of the horrors'. Educated conventionally at Eton and Trinity College, Cambridge, Leslie was destined for life as a Cambridge fellow, but during the early 1860s he gradually lost his faith; it was a crisis of conscience that put paid to his career as a Cambridge fellow, a profession for which one had to be ordained. Thus, he abandoned holy orders and his fellowship in 1862 and left Cambridge in 1864 to pursue a career as a journalist, literary critic, alpinist and philosophical writer, though he admitted to only having 'a good second class mind'. He wrote hundreds of articles for such diverse publications as *The Cornhill*, of which he became editor in 1871, *The Saturday Review*, *Fraser*, *Macmillan* and *The Fortnightly*. His most well-known works included *The History of English Thought in the Eighteenth Century* (1876 and 1881), and *The Science of Ethics* (1882) in which he supported Darwin's theory of evolution. However, Virginia, in recollections of her formidable father, did not find in him 'a subtle [...] imaginative [...] suggestive mind. But a strong mind; a healthy out of door, moor striding mind; an impatient, limited mind; a conventional mind'. Over the course of her writing life, Virginia would challenge and interrogate the work of her eminent yet emotionally unstable father, who she, most out of all his children, resembled. She wrote out her feelings for him in *To the Lighthouse* (1927), argued with him in her essays and mocked his style of biographical writing in *Orlando* (1928).

In 1867 Leslie married Harriet (Minnie) Thackeray, the youngest daughter of the great Victorian writer, William Makepeace Thackeray. Leslie represented Harriet as a child, an angel, his flower and his pet in *The Mausoleum Book*, written for his children as a series of sentimental recollections to be read after his demise. Sadly, his eight years of married happiness came to an abrupt end with her death in 1875 and he was left alone to bring up their daughter Laura, who suffered from severe mental health problems, surrounded by a gaggle of solicitous friends and relations, including his wife's flamboyant author-sister, Annie Ritchie. A year after his wife's death Leslie made the momentous decision to move to Hyde Park Gate in respectable Kensington. His next door neighbour was the beautiful, philanthropic and widowed Julia Duckworth (*née* Jackson). Julia Princep Jackson came from a long line of women noted for their good looks, a fact about which Virginia proudly speaks in her memoir papers. Virginia was also very proud of the aristocratic French lineage that her mother brought to the family. Her great-great-grand-parents included Thérèse Blin de Grincourt who had married Ambrose Pierre Antoine, Chevalier de L'Etang, a page at the court of Louis XIV and alleged lover of Marie Antoinette. During the French Revolution the Chevalier and his wife had fled to India where their daughter Adeline, Virginia's great-grandmother, had met and married James Pattle. Adeline and James produced seven daughters, who were known chiefly for their beauty and good natures, though one, Julia Margaret Cameron, became a notable photographer; Virginia Woolf eventually wrote her only play, *Freshwater*, about this particularly colourful great-aunt. In her introduction to an edition of Cameron's photographs, Virginia described the Pattles' milieu: 'they had the art of making round them, whether at Freshwater or at Little Holland House, a society of their own ("Pattledom" it was christened by Sir Henry Taylor), where they could drape and arrange, pull down and build up, and carry on life in a high-handed and adventurous way which painters and writers and even serious men of affairs found much to their liking.'[6] The fourth of these daughters, Maria Pattle, who married the prosaic Dr John Jackson, was Virginia's grandmother.

Their daughter Julia Princep Stephen, Virginia's mother, spent her youth at Little Holland House in Kensington with her aunt and uncle, Sarah and Thoby Princep, an environment that Virginia later imagined 'as a summer afternoon world'. It was a place where her mother was trained to worship the great men of the time, 'to pour out tea; to hand them their strawberries and cream; to listen devoutly, reverently to their wisdom; to accept the fact that Watts was the great painter; Tennyson the great poet; and to dance with the Prince of Wales'. Julia's portrait was painted by Edward Burne-Jones and Jacques-Émile Blanche, and she posed regularly for Julia Margaret Cameron. Leslie Stephen first met Julia Jackson at Little Holland House in the mid-1860s, but she was soon married to the barrister Herbert Duckworth in 1867 having turned down proposals from the painters William Holman Hunt and Thomas Woolner. The Duckworths' marriage was idyllic; Virginia records the impressions gleaned about this union from snippets of information fed to her by friends and relations, characterising it as full of 'the golden enchantments of Tennysonian sentiment'. With Herbert Duckworth, Julia had three children: George born 1868, Stella born 1869, and Gerald born after his father's untimely death in 1870.

On the death of Herbert Duckworth, Julia's grief was so intense that she would lie, according to anecdote, upon his grave at Orchardleigh, near Frome, Somerset, and at just twenty-four years old abandoned her faith and cloaked the rest of her character in a deep melancholy. Thereafter, she, as Virginia put it, 'pressed the bitterest fruit only to her lips. She visited the poor, nursed the dying, and felt herself possessed of the true secret of life at last [...] that sorrow is our lot, and at best we can but face it bravely.' At the same time, this loss made her supremely practical and she was a welcome nurse at sick beds, even writing the short essay 'Notes from Sick Rooms' (1883) in which she demonstrates a startling sensitivity to the emotional as well as practical needs of the infirm. She had visited the Stephens regularly before Minnie's death and helped to nurse her in her last illness; it was perhaps Leslie's grief, similar to Julia's own, and his agnosticism (she had read and approved of his 'An Agnostic's Apology' published in the *Fortnightly Review* in 1876) that eventually made him a suitable match. Leslie recorded his impressions of his beautiful widowed neighbour in *The Mausoleum Book*; she was his angel in the house, selfless and sympathetic to a fault. He asked Julia to marry him several times, but she eventually agreed by quietly stating on his departure from an evening visit to her house that she would try to be a good wife to him. They were married in 1878 and had four children in quick succession, though the last seems to have been an unplanned pregnancy. Vanessa arrived on 30th May 1879, Julian Thoby on 9th August 1880, Adeline Virginia on 25th January 1882 and Adrian on 27th October 1883 (the youngest son was, as Virginia recalls, their mother's favourite and was often left out of his older siblings' games). Of her parents' marriage Virginia was certain that each 'found in the other the highest and most perfect harmony which their natures could respond to' and she immortalised their union in her 1927 novel, *To the Lighthouse*, in the characters of Mr and Mrs Ramsay.

The large Stephen family lived at 22 Hyde Park Gate, which was located in a quiet cul-de-sac of respectable Kensington. Initially a small Victorian town house, it was extended and added to as the size and needs of the family changed; Julia Stephen sketched her own designs for the house to save on architects' fees. The house contained not only Leslie and Julia Stephen and their four children, but the three Duckworth children by Julia's first marriage and, until around 1892, Leslie's daughter by his first marriage to Minnie Thackeray, Laura. Her erratic behaviour and incoherent chatter eventually led to her incarceration at an asylum in York. Several servants were required to run this household which had no plumbed water or electricity – Virginia recalled the smell of candle grease on the first floor and the brass hot water cans sitting by the 'solitary family bath' a few years later. The house itself was represented by Virginia as a living presence, 'tangled and matted with emotion'. She vividly re-called the atmosphere at 22 Hyde Park Gate: the house swathed in Virginia creeper and covered in red plush; her father reading or reciting poetry; her mother presiding over the tea table or rushing out to help at sick beds. The visitors who graced this Victorian pile with their presence included some of the most notable intellectual and artistic figures of the day: Henry James, Elizabeth Robins, John Addington Symonds, Philip Burne-Jones, George Meredith, G.F. Watts, Henry Sidgwick, R.B. Haldane, John Morley. The children were kept at the top of the house in the night nursery which became Virginia's room as a teenager. Vanessa Bell reflected many years later that it 'must by modern standards have been a very unhealthy atmosphere'.[7] Here the Stephen children ate, washed and slept, coming downstairs for lessons with their parents and private tutors. In bed at night Virginia would weave elaborate tales to amuse her sister and brothers, usually about the rich Dilke family who lived next door. When older, the Stephens and Duckworths would meet for meals and for teatime, over which Julia, as matriarch, and Stella Duckworth, as her beautiful lieutenant, would preside. Of the tea table, Virginia said: 'It was like watching a game. One had to know the rules.' The drawing room was divided by a set of black folding doors which allowed for some degree of privacy in a family of nine. 'On one side of the door,' Virginia recalled, in '22 Hyde Park Gate':

Cousin Adeline, Duchess of Bedford, perhaps would be on her knees – the Duke had died tragically at Woburn; Mrs Dolmetsch would be telling how she had found her husband in bed with the parlour-maid or Lisa Stillman would be sobbing that Walter Headlam had chalked her nose with a billiard cue [...]

Though dark and agitated on one side, the other side of the door, especially on Sunday afternoons, was cheerful enough. There round the oval tea table with its pink china shell full of spice buns would be found old General Beadle, talking of the Indian Mutiny; or Mr Haldane, or Sir Frederick Pollock – talking of all things under the sun; or old C.B. Clarke, whose name is given to three excessively rare Himalayan ferns; and Professor Wolstenholme, capable, if you interrupted him, of spouting two columns of tea not unmixed with sultanas through his nostrils; after which he would relapse into a drowsy ursine torpor, the result of eating opium to which he had been driven by the unkindness of his wife and the untimely death of his son Oliver who was eaten, somewhere off the coast of Coromandel, by a shark.

When Virginia reflected on the house she became 'suffocated' by it and claimed: 'I could write the history of every mark and scratch [...] The walls and the rooms had in sober truth been built to our shape.'

When Vanessa recalled her sister as a child of this house, she recollected 'a very rosy chubby baby, with bright green eyes, sitting in a high chair at the nursery table, drumming impatiently for her breakfast'.[8] Virginia was the favourite 'pet' of her father who, in letters, would write: 'My love to all the pets, specially to my Ginia – I have been thinking of her all day'.[9] However, the most convincing sketches of her childhood and adolescence at 22 Hyde Park Gate are by her own hand, not only in her memoir papers, but also in her fiction. Childhood consisted, in her memory, of 'Many bright colours; many distinct sounds; some human beings, caricatures; comic; several violent moments of being, always including a circle of the scene which they cut out: and all surrounded by a vast space'. She recalled it largely unfolding in the drawing room, nursery and in Kensington Gardens while in London, but also in the family's holiday home, Talland House in St Ives, Cornwall. Though her London childhood at Hyde Park Gate was strictly regulated and likened variously to a cage, a circus tent and a fish tank, the family's summer holidays at St Ives represented 'rapture'. St Ives evoked a feeling of such happiness and calm that Virginia consistently returned to it in her fiction; and in her memory it was a place that she could 'go back to [...] more completely than [...] this morning'. Leslie Stephen found the house on one of his many walking tours and, despite the inconvenience of the location, he bought the lease and transported the family there every year from 1882 to 1894. Some of her happiest memories are linked to those summers where the family would break the strict regulation of their London hours to play cricket, take photographs, sugar the trees in order to catch moths (a favourite pastime) and take boat trips to the lighthouse; but, even in St Ives, the family entertained numerous visitors and her mother did not break her routine of visiting the poor and attending sick beds. In 1905, many years after their mother's death, and the year after their father's, the Stephen children returned to look at the house; it was a surreal and melancholy experience, though they were delighted to find themselves, and particularly their mother, remembered there with affection. This vivid memory of a happy childhood spent at Talland House re-surfaces in her fiction: *Jacob's Room* (1922), *To the Lighthouse* (1927) and *The Waves* (1932). All of these novels draw on specific images which are linked in her diaries and memoirs to this time. It was, she admitted, 'the best beginning to life conceivable'.

However much St Ives may haunt the pages of Virginia's later novels, many of the reasons for Virginia's success as a writer, and her sister Vanessa's as a painter, had to do with their adolescence in the dimly lit rooms of Hyde Park Gate. Vanessa recalled in her 1948 Memoir Club paper, 'Notes on Virginia's Childhood', that she could not 'remember a time when Virginia did not mean to be a writer and I a painter. It was a lucky arrangement, for it meant that we went our own ways and one source of jealousy at any rate was absent'.[10] Virginia's feminist agendas were also established there alongside her literary ambitions. The stifling example set to the sisters by their mother and older half-sister, who were living embodiements of Victorian 'angels in the house' and thus actively against women's suffrage (Julia signed a petition appealing against it), was anathema to Virginia and Vanessa Stephen. It was an identity that Virginia eventually attacked and came to kill in her later feminist works: *A Room of One's Own* (1929) and *Three Guineas* (1938) and the lecture 'Professions for Women' (1931). This interest in the discrepancy between the male and female situation was also made more evident by the consciousness that their brothers Thoby and Adrian were afforded a public-school and Cambridge education, while the sisters were tutored erratically at home. Their teachers included Julia and

Leslie Stephen; their older half-sister Stella; and private tutors for Greek and Latin, including Dr Warr of King's College, London, Clara Pater and Janet Case. However, both sisters did also attend a variety of courses at King's College, which undermines somewhat Virginia's claims to have had no formal education. Virginia lived vicariously through Thoby's schooling; her letters are full of reverence for his superior knowledge and desires to have her opinions vetted and approved. She called him 'your highness' and was delighted to hear from Vanessa that 'he thought [she] might be a bit of a genius' – the sisters vied for his attention and praise. It was partly this marked difference in education and expectations that ushered the sisters into proving themselves with more energy than might otherwise have been the case.

Sir Leslie Stephen was strangely supportive of his daughters' artistic aims. He allowed Vanessa to study art, which she did under the tutorage of, variously, Ebenezer Cooke, John Macallan Swan, John Singer Sargent and Henry Tonks. She attended Cope's School of Art between 1896 and 1900 and won a place at the prestigious Royal Academy Schools in 1901. With Virginia (Ginia or Ginny as he preferred to call her), he simply opened the doors of his library, only exclaiming occasionally at her voracity for reading: 'Gracious child, how you gobble!' He stated in a letter to Julia on 29th July 1893 when Virginia was just eleven: 'She takes in a great deal and will really be an author in time', though he undermined this impression of forward thinking somewhat by deeming this to be 'a thing for ladies and Ginia will do well in that line'.[11] Both Julia and he applauded her writing in the family newspaper *The Hyde Park Gate News*, which was almost exclusively her own work. 'How excited I used to be when the "Hyde Park Gate News" was laid on her plate on Monday morning, and she liked something I had written! Never shall I forget my extremity of pleasure'. It contained a variety of reports on family duties, visits, theatre trips, games and several imaginative pieces. She also wrote, or related, stories to her parents presenting them for much-needed approval. 'It was like being a violin and being played upon –' she recalled, 'when I found that she [Julia Stephen] had sent a story of mine to Madge Symonds; it was so imaginative, she said; it was about souls flying round and choosing bodies to be born into.'

The Stephen sisters pursued their goals with an inimitable single-mindedness and determination, though their personal passions were interrupted of course by their position as dutiful daughters and wives in training. Both sisters recalled with agony having to down pen, book and brush to help preside over the tea table around which awkward young men would sit in silence and be coaxed into speech. It was their job to make guests feel comfortable, 'silence', she observed, 'was a breach of convention'. Although a time of awkwardness and pain for the sisters, the older Virginia did give this 'tea table training' some credit for her ability 'to slip in [to her writing] things that would be inaudible if one marched straight up and spoke out loud'. It was this shared and confined experience of life at Hyde Park Gate that solidified the 'close conspiracy' between the sisters. Virginia consistently characterized the beautiful Vanessa Stephen as the strong, stable, mother-figure, whom she nicknamed Saint and Dolphin, while she would play the childish and precocious Goat, Billy, Capra, Miss Jan or Singes. This arrangement was not always appreciated; as Vanessa admitted, Virginia was 'not very old when speech became the deadliest weapon as used by her' and Vanessa records her feelings at being reduced to 'the misery of sarcasm from the grown-ups' after Virginia labelled her 'The Saint'.[12] Their relationship was complex; deeply loving, yet filled with rivalry. Rivalry over how fast their plants were growing; rivalry for the attention of their beloved brother Thoby; rivalry over the gifts they were given by their 'sponsors' (the children were not christened, so they were given sponsors rather than godparents; Virginia's was the American Ambassador, James Russell Lowell). Vanessa's claim that 'one source of jealousy was absent' from their choices of career was only partly true, for when Vanessa was given an easel to stand at, Virginia demanded a lectern to write at fearing that her writing might be deemed less strenuous and therefore the lesser art. Nevertheless, Virginia's admiration and love for her older sister is evident in her fiction in which she re-imagined Vanessa as the independent Katharine Hilbery of *Night and Day* (1919), the earthy Susan of *The Waves* (1931) and the practical Maggie Pargiter of *The Years* (1937).

Virginia's childhood, though strictly regulated, had been largely happy but this childhood idyll ended abruptly at the age of thirteen on 5th May 1895 when Julia Princep Stephen died at just forty-eight years old of rheumatic fever. The room in which she died was the same in which all four of the Stephen children were born, 'was the sexual centre; the birth centre, the death centre of the house'. Virginia recalled her mother's last words to her on that night many years later: 'Hold yourself straight, my little Goat,' she said to her terrified daughter. When she was taken into the room to kiss her mother goodbye she saw how her father 'staggered from the bedroom as we came'. 'I stretched out my arms to stop him,' she remembered, 'but he brushed past me, crying out something I could not catch; distraught' – this image, which remained so vividly in her memory, is repeated in her penultimate novel, *The Years*, over forty years later. Recalling the moments after her mother's death, Virginia concluded 'she was the centre; it was herself [...] For after that day there was nothing left of it [...] everything had come to an end.' At the centre of the well of grief was Leslie Stephen, making emotional demands for sympathy that ignored the claims of any others to their own sadness and pity. 'There was something in the darkened rooms, the groans, the passionate lamentations that passed the normal limits of sorrow, and hung about the genuine tragedy with folds of Eastern drapery.' It was he whom the children began to blame for their mother's death, he had worn her out with his petty demands and irritability, and even he enquired of his behaviour to Julia: 'I was not as bad as Carlyle, was I?'

It was this cataclysmic event that precipitated Virginia's first mental breakdown, signs of which were present in the family's history of mental illness and in her anxiousness during early childhood. Her own opinions of madness or 'idiocy', like her anti-Semitic comments, are unpleasant to modern readers. Perhaps fearful of being equated to her mentally deficient half-sister Laura, Virginia took a dim view of it. On a walk in 1915 for example she 'had to pass a long line of imbeciles [...] every one in that long line was a miserable ineffective shuffling idiotic creature, with no forehead, or no chin, & an imbecile grin, or a wild suspicious stare. It was perfectly horrible. They should certainly be killed' – perhaps attack was the best form of defence. The cures for her subsequent mental traumas included long and unwelcome walks with her father; a cocktail of drugs; visits to stay with relations and weeks in rest homes. Her chief pleasures, reading and writing, were often curtailed and she was forced to drink endless glasses of milk; it was also thought that the problem might be related to her teeth and she had many of them pulled out in later life as a consequence. Many years later it was a topic that caused much pain in the recalling: 'It was a subject that I have kept cooling in my mind until I felt I could touch it without bursting into flame all over. You can't think what a raging furnace it is still to me – madness and doctors and being forced. But let's change the subject.' However, more interestingly, in a 1930 letter to Ethel Smyth she hinted, with a degree of flippancy, that her past madness was the source of much of her creative output: 'As an experience, madness is terrific I can assure you, and not to be sniffed at; and in its lava I still find most of the things I write about. It shoots out of one everything shaped, final, not in mere driblets, as sanity does.' In this letter she seems to suggest that madness and genius do indeed go hand in hand, but this statement is unusual and most of the time her mental problems were laughed off by both herself and the rest of the family: she was 'Mad Aunt Virginia' to her nieces and nephews, while the adults merely quipped, 'Everyone knows the goat's mad.'

After Julia's death, the family entered into 'a period of Oriental gloom' and it was Virginia's older half-sister Stella Duckworth who stepped into the void left by their mother. Stella unquestioningly took on the mantle of housekeeper and continued Julia's philanthropic work: looking after her younger siblings; visiting Leslie's disabled daughter, Laura; going to the workhouse; or overseeing her cottages. She uncomplainingly supported her grieving stepfather while hiding her own sorrow in household duties and the care of others. Stella presents a very tragic figure in Woolf's recollections; she is characterized as 'very gentle, very honest', with 'charm', 'modesty', 'unselfishness', 'lack of pose', 'lack of snobbery'. Virginia spoke about her as an 'elderblossom'; 'large white roses'; or 'a white faint moon in a blue sky'. She was very beautiful, as photographs attest, very passive and very pale.

In 1896 Stella Duckworth became engaged to her most persistent suitor, John Waller Hills. Jack, as he was known to the family, offered Stella the chance to escape from the demands of her stepfather whose grief at Julia's death overshadowed all else. There were 'scenes' when Stella became engaged and more 'scenes' when she finally found the courage to tell her stepfather that she and Jack would not be setting up home at 22 Hyde Park Gate. In the year of Stella's marriage to Jack, Virginia began to keep a diary which she wrote almost all of her life; it is in this notebook that she recorded her fifteenth year and the terrible events that marred it. Shortly after returning from her honeymoon, Stella was taken ill with 'a bad chill on her innards'. The illness seemed to abate, but kept resurfacing for the subsequent three months until she died after an operation to treat peritonitis on 27th July 1897. Virginia remembered Stella's death as 'a night-mare' which destroyed the moment of joy and renewal that Stella's marriage to Jack had briefly symbolised. The diary that Virginia was keeping at this time stops after Stella's death with the words 'it is impossible to write of' and is resumed two days later, but only to record simple events told in broken and brief sentences. She wrote in this diary of feeling 'very strange & unhappy', 'silent & miserable [...] & lonely'. 'Life is a hard business,' she reflected, 'one needs a rhinirocerous skin – & that one has not got.' Again, it was Leslie who Virginia and Vanessa blamed for Stella's death: he had 'tasked Stella's strength, embittered her few months of joy'. To Virginia's horror 'he was quite prepared to take Vanessa for his next victim' and her memoirs recall how her beloved older sister would stand the blasts of Leslie's rage while she cowered speechless and unable to intervene. 'When he was sad, he explained, she should be sad; when he was angry, as he was periodically when she asked him for a cheque, she should weep; instead she stood before him like a stone.' He became 'the tyrant father – the exacting, the violent, the histrionic, the demonstrative, the self-centred, the self pitying, the deaf, the appealing, the alternately loved and hated father [...] It was like being shut up in the same cage with a wild beast.' Vanessa never forgave her father for his use of her after Stella's death, though Virginia, perhaps because of the similarities between them, was more tolerant of his flaws in later life.

In the year following Stella's death the family moved as if in a trance, trying to regain some sense of normality. Jack Hills, Stella's bereft husband, haunted the drawing room and his reliance on the sympathy of Vanessa and Virginia was intense. However, his conversations with Vanessa soon began to take a different, more romantic turn, and there was talk of, what would have been at that time, a scandalous marriage – it was against British law to marry a dead sibling's spouse. The Duckworth brothers anxiously appealed to their stepfather to intervene and in a moment of temperance he stated that she must 'please herself', much to Virginia's pleasure and surprise. Eventually, the potential liaison petered out and other suitors were sought; George Duckworth (like Gerald to a lesser extent) was particularly keen to launch Vanessa and Virginia on to the marriage market and he took them, reluctantly on their part, under his wing. George tried desperately to make his beautiful half-sisters a social success, though as Virginia records in various amusing recollections, this task was largely unsuccessful. 'The truth of it is, […]' she confided in a letter to Emma Vaughan, 'we are failures. Really, we can't shine in Society. I don't know how it's done. We aint popular – we sit in corners and look like mutes who are longing for a funeral.' Previous experiences of the brothers' affection were not favourable; Virginia recalled an incident in very early childhood where Gerald 'began to explore [her] body'. She described in 'A Sketch of the Past':

the feel of his hand going under my clothes; going firmly and steadily lower and lower. I remember how I hoped that he would stop; how I stiffened and wriggled as his hand approached my private parts. But it did not stop. His hand explored my private parts too. I remember resenting, disliking it – what is the word for so dumb and mixed a feeling? It must have been strong, since I still recall it.

It is unclear what the brothers did physically to their half-sisters in later years, though enough is hinted at to provoke unpleasant speculations. Her memoir paper '22 Hyde Park Gate' was the most explicit in this regard; it is here that she stated: 'the old ladies of Kensington and Belgravia never knew that George Duckworth was not only father and mother, brother and sister to those poor Stephen girls; he was their lover also.' And she records in a letter of 1911 to her sister, Janet Case's reaction to 'all Georges malefactions'. 'To my surprise, she has always had an intense dislike of him; and used to say "Whew – you nasty creature", when he came in and began fondling me over my Greek. When I got to the bedroom scenes, she dropped her lace, and gasped like a benevolent gudgeon.'

Once their mother and Stella had died, George Duckworth began to introduce Vanessa properly into society. He bestowed on her a variety of fabulous gifts, from 'a wonderful *opal necklace*' which, according to Virginia's diary, was her 'envy' and 'delight', to an Arab mare. When Vanessa finally refused point blank to accompany him to any more parties he took Virginia instead, reviewing her appearance each evening before departure; one such 'appraisal' heard him tell her to tear up her dress. Her memories of this adolescence more generally were later distilled into one unpleasant image: 'while father preserved the framework of 1860, George filled in the framework with all kinds of minutely-teethed saws; and the machine into which our rebellious bodies were inserted in 1900 not only held us tight in its framework, but bit into us with innumerable sharp teeth.' If her experience of living with Leslie Stephen was like being shut up with a caged beast, then her time living under the same roof as George Duckworth was like being 'shut up in the same tank with an unwieldy and turbulent whale'.

All through these difficult years following her mother's and Stella's deaths, Virginia kept up an impressive reading and writing regime. Her diaries and notebooks from 1895 to 1904 contain reading lists covering the whole gamut of world literature, ancient and modern; as well as biography, history, travel writing and natural science. 'Reading four books at once,' she boasted in January 1897. Virginia, like many voracious teenage readers, was not allowed to continue her reading into the night and had to 'shut up' her book on the French Revolution 'in the middle of [her] nightly forbidden reading' for fear that George might be coming to check on her. 'However,' she noted, much relieved, 'it was a false alarm, & the 1st vol. was finished.' To Virginia Stephen, in the midst of death and social embarrassment, books were 'the greatest help and comfort' and it was at this time, she vividly recalled in 'Reminiscences', that words suddenly became living things:

I remember going into Kensington Gardens about that time. It was a hot spring evening, and we lay down – Nessa and I – in the long grass behind the Flower Walk. I had taken *The Golden Treasury* with me. I opened it and began to read some poem. And instantly and for the first time I understood the poem (which it was I forget). It was as if it became altogether intelligible; I had a feeling of transparency in words when they cease to be words and become so intensified that one seems to experience them; to foretell them as if they developed what one is already feeling. I was so astonished that I tried to explain the feeling. 'One seems to understand what it's about', I said awkwardly. I suppose Nessa has forgotten; no one could have understood from what I said the queer feeling I had in the hot grass, that poetry was coming true. Nor does that give the feeling. It matches what I have sometimes felt when I write. The pen gets on the scent.

Virginia also, as this extract suggests, began her 'apprenticeship' in writing in these years. She often first tested phrases and images out in her diary, such as in an entry dated 7th August 1899 in which she 'expound[ed] another simile that ha[d] been rolling itself round in [her] mind'; or when she reflected that 'such a relation of details is extraordinarily difficult, dull & unprofitable to read. However there is no end to writing, & each time I hope that I may make better stuff of it.' The diary, and even the letters, were throughout her life places where ideas and styles could have a trial run before being aired carefully in her fiction. Her early notebook dating from 1903 also contains thirty short writing exercises treating subjects as diverse as dancing in 'A Dance in Queens Gate' to 'The Wilton Carpet Factory'; from a description called simply 'Miss Case' about her Greek tutor to a rhapsody entitled 'The Beginning of the Storm'. Of course neither father nor brothers were safe to present these immature pieces of work to and so she cast about for a suitable and reliable critic on which to throw her early experiments.

Virginia's relationships with women at this time were deep and passionate. Perhaps they were so because of the loss of her mother and older half-sister, or perhaps they offered a remedy to the unwanted attentions of her father and half-brothers. Duncan Grant recalled when he met her in the early 1900s that 'there was always something a little aloof and even a little fierce in her manner to most men'.[13] Most of the women to whom she formed an attachment were at least ten years older than she. The most notable of these friendships included Emma Vaughan (nicknamed Toad), Madge Vaughan (*née* Symonds), who was the daughter of the writer John Addington Symonds, and the motherly Violet Dickinson. To these women, Virginia wrote, often a letter a day. It was on them that she tried out her various personae and through them that she cultivated an epistolary style that was both amusing and vicious. She also sent these women snippets of her writing for criticism, perhaps expecting softer treatment and greater admiration at their hands than at the hands of father and brothers. After a boating accident, for example, Virginia wrote a comic account which she sent to Emma Vaughan for feedback: 'I have written a long account of our great accident; and I expect a very nice letter to thank me. Do you see? You must read my work carefully – not missing my peculiar words – and then tell me your criticisms and humble thanks.' Not only did she seek their approval and advice about her writing, she also immortalised these women and her feelings for them in her fiction. Her almost erotic feelings for the glamorous aspiring writer Madge Vaughan, recalled in a later diary entry of 1921, were reincarnated in the character of Sally Seton in her 1925 novel *Mrs Dalloway*. Like Sally Seton, Madge became a bourgeois matriarch, though married unhappily to a schoolmaster rather than a merchant. However, her most intimate relationship at this time, other than the unique bond with her sister, was with the 'harumscarum' Violet Dickinson. Violet was a spinster of six feet tall; welcome in some of the foremost families of England, including the Cecils and the Bath family; and always ready to offer support and advice on any number of unusual and diverse subjects, from children to greenfly, from husbands to beeswax. Their intimacy grew in the years after

Stella's death. It was to Violet that Virginia confided the real state of her dour family life and her dislike of the Duckworth brothers; and it was to her that she sent most of her earliest stories and sketches for approval. From Violet she demanded a peculiar blend of erotic and motherly affection. She called it a 'romantic friendship'; she demanded 'hot and affectionate' letters; she was the bird Sparroy who was 'very much attached'; she was a baby wallaby who wished to find refuge in Violet's pouch; she asked for advice and sounded out her own turbulent personality against the safe and solid one of her friend. Violet was one of the first to realise how far Virginia might take her writing, and Vanessa relayed Violet's words about her sister to Virginia in a letter of 1904: 'she thinks your writing most wonderful [...] She thought you would undoubtedly be a great writer one day. Your things are so well thought out – fresh and original and interesting. You always have something to say on any subject and your writing is so living. Is that enough for you? She really thinks you a genius.' To Violet herself Virginia confided, 'You are the person I can best stand criticism from', and even demanded an opinion on her epistolary style: 'Do you like my fluent rounded style, or my curt and mordant style the best?' She was the subject of Virginia's 1907 sketch, 'Friendships Gallery'. However, her feelings for these women faded quickly after her father's death, they seemed to symbolise an old life that his end was to leave behind. Nevertheless, it was to Violet that Virginia turned when her father's health began to fail and it was her help in its aftermath that in many ways saved her life.

Sir Leslie Stephen began to decline after a fainting fit in 1900 and two years later he was diagnosed with terminal bowel cancer. Initially reluctant to admit defeat at the hands of the disease, Sir Leslie finally succumbed to his illness and died on 22nd February 1904, leaving his exhausted and relieved children to carve their own paths in the world. It seemed to Virginia at this time that there was 'Nothing in this world but deaths and illnesses' and she became increasingly frustrated with the well-meant, but fruitless solicitations of 'swarming' relations. 'I liken them to all kinds of parasitic animals etc etc:' she lamented to Violet, 'really I think they deserve no better. Three mornings have I spent having my hand held, and my emotions pumped out of me, quite unsuccessfully. They are good people, I know, but it would be merciful if they could keep their virtues and affections and all the rest of it to themselves'. As her father lay dying, plans were afoot to move the remaining family to the disreputable bohemian area of Bloomsbury. Virginia wrote to Violet: 'Jack [Hills] went with us, sensible but discouraging, showed us the neighbourhood which he thinks bad and says we should never get anybody to come and see us, or to dine.' Jack's reaction to the house hunting seems to have been the standard response of the Stephens' respectable family and friends; even Violet had her reservations. After her father's death, Virginia wrote to Violet about her guilt and her grief: 'The dreadful thing is that I never did enough for him all those years. He was so lonely often, and I never helped him as I might have done. This is the worst part of it now. If he had only lived we could have been so happy. But it is all gone.'

For Virginia, her father's death was mentally devastating and she lapsed into madness for several months during which time she stayed with Violet at her home, Burnham Wood, near Welwyn, where she first attempted suicide by throwing herself out of a window. Later she visited her aunt Caroline Emilia Stephen in Cambridge who, Virginia wrote in a letter to Violet, 'maddens me when she begins to talk about Father', and finally she spent some weeks with Madge and Will Vaughan at Giggleswick in Yorkshire. Her frustration at these months of convalescence in the houses of others was compounded by the knowledge that her siblings were arranging to leave their old life in Hyde Park Gate and were to move to 46 Gordon Square, Bloomsbury without her help. Her anger at being kept away again found vent in letters to Violet:

I cant make her, or you, or anybody, see that it is a great hardship to me to have to spend two more long months wandering about in other peoples comfortless houses, when I have my own house [Gordon Square] waiting for me and rent paid regular on Quarter day [...] They dont realise that London means my own home, and books, and pictures, and music, from all of which I have been parted since February now, – and I have never spent such a wretched 8 months in my life. And yet that tyrannical, and as I think, shortsighted [Dr] Savage insists upon another two. I told him when I saw him that the only place I can be quiet and free is in my home, with Nessa: [...] I long for a large room to myself, with books and nothing else, where I can shut myself up, and see no one, and read myself into peace. This would be possible at Gordon Sq: and nowhere else. I wonder why Savage doesn't see this.

However, once recovered, this move, combined with the death of her demanding father, gave Virginia the freedom she needed to begin developing as a writer. It is no coincidence that her first article appeared on 7th December 1904, nine months after her father's death. In this year she also dutifully assisted Frederic Maitland in writing the *Life and Letters of Sir Leslie Stephen* (1906) because, as her sister Vanessa told her, 'you understood Father better than anyone else did'. Sadly (and unfairly) for Sir Leslie Stephen he is most devastatingly remembered by his gifted daughter in a 1928 diary entry: 'Father's birthday. He would have been 1928 1832 96 96, yes, today; & could have been 96, like other people one has known; but mercifully was not. His life would have entirely ended mine. What would have happened? No writing, no books; – inconceivable.'

Bloomsbury

On 1st January 1905, the Stephen children were celebrating Christmas and New Year in the New Forest. 'This is at any rate a cheerful New Years day,' Virginia recorded in her diary, 'as though we had turned over a new leaf & swept the sky clean of clouds' and two days later noted, 'Read, wrote, cursed, & walked – all as usual.' On 14th January she went to see Dr Savage 'who was well satisfied' with her health. He 'thinks me "normal"' she confided to her diary, '& able to return to all my usual ways, going out, work, &c – so that horrible long illness which began in the 2nd week of April last year, is now fairly put away, & I need think no more of it'. The months of mental illness and itinerant convalescence were over, the prospect of a new life at 46 Gordon Square, Bloomsbury, was beckoning. 'Really Gordon Square with the lamps lit and the light on the green,' she wrote to the sceptical Violet Dickinson, 'is a romantic place'. It was also the beginning of her career as a reviewer, which had tentatively started in November 1904 with Mrs Margaret Lyttelton, editor of the Women's Supplement of *The Guardian*. On 14th December 1904 a review of *The Son of Royal Langbrith* by W.D. Howells appeared, followed by an essay on the Brontës at Haworth on 21st December. Virginia was delighted with her earnings almost as much as with her writing itself: 'Found this morning on my plate my first instalment of wages – £2.7.6. for Guardian articles, which gave me great pleasure.' In January 1905 she met Bruce

Richmond, editor of *The Times Literary Supplement,* with a view to writing for him, and by 23rd February she was bragging to Emma Vaughan:

> I am writing for – now for my boast –
> The Times Lit. Supplement.
> The Academy
> The National Review
> The Guardian –

On 14th March 1905 she was joyfully lamenting 'Another book from the Times! – a fat novel, I'm sorry to say. They pelt me now.' Indeed, over the course of her career, Virginia produced hundreds of articles for magazines, newspapers and journals on a wide range of topics.

Her sister was similarly busy with her painting and Vanessa's portrait of Lady Robert Cecil was shown in the 18th Summer Exhibition of Works by Living Artists at the New Gallery in 1905. In the following years Vanessa went on to exhibit with the New English Art Club, the Allied Artists Association and the Friday Club, but her first solo exhibition did not take place until 1922 at the Independent Gallery. Vanessa's desire to innovate was outlined clearly in a letter to Margery Snowdon dated 11th January 1905: 'the moment one imitates other people one's done for. It's allowable while one's a student, learning the language and trying to find out what one does think of it all, but when one once starts alone one must be oneself.' Now free from the edicts of their Victorian family and armed with an impressive work ethic and a desire to create something new in art and literature, it seemed that their plans to become writer and painter respectively were beginning to take flight. As Virginia claimed to Violet in January 1905: 'I want to work like a steam engine', and on holiday in Cornwall later that year, Virginia wrote to Emma Vaughan that 'Nessa paints all the afternoon; and I write all the morning.'

It was really Vanessa's formidable determination that propelled the orphaned Stephens into a new and more avant-garde life in Bloomsbury. After Sir Leslie's death she immediately set about cutting ties with the older generation and those members of the family who represented the repressive elements of their youth. George and Gerald Duckworth were particularly put out by this quite systematic attempt to expunge them along with the rest. In her Memoir Club paper, 'Old Bloomsbury', Virginia recalled: '[Vanessa] had sold; she had burnt; she had sorted; she had torn up [...] The four of us were therefore left alone. And Vanessa – looking at a map of London and seeing how far apart they were – had decided that we should leave Kensington and start life afresh in Bloomsbury.' Gone were the G.F. Watts paintings, gone was the Venetian tradition, 'everything was going to be new; everything was going to be different. Everything was on trial.' They travelled widely to Italy, France, Spain, Greece; they talked freely of bodily functions; insisted on using Christian names; smoked cigarettes; refused to dress for dinner; stayed up late debating philosophy; and were eventually unguarded enough to confront the sticky subject of sex. Virginia comically recalled the moment when the taboos governing this topic came down:

Suddenly the door opened and the long and sinister figure of Mr Lytton Strachey stood on the threshold. He pointed his finger at a stain on Vanessa's white dress.

'Semen?' he said.

Can one really say it? I thought and we burst out laughing. With that one word all barriers of reticence and reserve went down. A flood of the sacred fluid seemed to overwhelm us. Sex permeated our conversation. [...]

So there was now nothing that one could not say, nothing that one could not do, at 46 Gordon Square. It was, I think, a great advance in civilisation.

The Stephens became the nucleus of what came to be known, sometimes pejoratively, as 'The Bloomsbury Group'. Bloomsbury was, of course, the area from which the group took its name, though it was not a coherent organisation as the word 'group' seems to suggest. In his autobiography, Leonard Woolf explained that the term Bloomsbury was 'applied to a largely imaginary group of persons with largely imaginary objects and characteristics. I was a member of this group and I was also one of a small number of persons who did in fact eventually form a kind of group of friends living in or around that district of London legitimately called Bloomsbury.'[14] Leonard goes on to list these people as Vanessa, Virginia and Adrian Stephen, Clive Bell, Lytton Strachey, John Maynard Keynes, Duncan Grant, E.M. Forster, Saxon Sydney-Turner, Roger Fry, Desmond and Molly MacCarthy and himself, and then later Angelica, Julian and Quentin Bell and David (Bunny) Garnett. He also considers it to have come into being after his return from Ceylon, but the beginnings of it were established much earlier in 1905 after his departure for a civil service position in Ceylon (now Sri Lanka) in 1904. The original collection of family and friends were centred around the Stephen siblings and Thoby's Cambridge friends: Lytton, Saxon and Clive, the latter of whom, like Thoby, had not been elected to the prestigious 'secret' Cambridge society, The Apostles. The Apostles and Cambridge also connected the group with a wider circle of thinkers and writers: the philosopher Bertrand Russell, the economist John Maynard Keynes, the writer E.M. Forster and the philosopher G.E. Moore, whose *Principia Ethica* influenced the group's moral and ethical outlooks.

Initially the grouping was awkward and uncomfortable; Virginia wrote to Violet about them: 'They sit silent, absolutely silent, all the time; occasionally they escape to a corner & chuckle over a Latin joke [...] Oh women are my line and not these inanimate creatures'; and in a later comic reminiscence she recalled:

They came in hesitatingly, self-effacingly, and folded themselves up quietly [in] the corners of sofas. For a long time
they said nothing. None of our old conversational openings
seemed to do […] The conversation languished in a way that
would have been impossible in the drawing room at Hyde
Park Gate. Yet the silence was difficult, not dull. It seemed
as if the standard of what was worth saying had risen so
high that it was better not to break it unworthily. We sat
and looked at the ground. Then at last Vanessa, having said
perhaps that she had been to some picture show, incau-
tiously used the word 'beauty'. At that, one of the young
men would lift his head slowly and say, 'It depends what you
mean by beauty.' At once all our ears were pricked. It was
as if the bull had at last been turned into the ring.

The bull might be 'beauty', might be 'good', might be
'reality'. Whatever it was, it was some abstract question that
now drew out all our forces.

At first intimidated by this requirement to speak seriously about
intellectual conundrums and weighted down with a desire to
impress, Virginia was soon coming home to find 'Bell, & we
talked the nature of good till almost one!' They set up Thursday
Evenings for the discussion of ideas; the first of these took place
on 16th March 1905. In October 1905 Vanessa launched The Friday
Club, which was formed to discuss and exhibit the fine arts. Of
the first exhibition Virginia wrote to Violet: 'it was successful,
I think, except that the room was small and dingy and dark, and
we had to carry round lamps when the light gave out. But I think
people were interested in the pictures, and there were no very
bad ones. Nessa's showed up well.' Eventually, the sisters were
introduced by Lytton Strachey to his cousin, the painter Duncan
Grant, with whom Vanessa, several years later, entered into a love
affair and a lifelong artistic collaboration.

'Love was never mentioned,' according to Virginia in her
recollections of 'Old Bloomsbury'. 'It seemed incredible,' she

remembered, 'that any of these young men should want to marry us or that we should want to marry them.' Even at this early stage she realised that marriage was a destiny tottering precariously over them all: 'I could feel a horrible necessity impending over us; a fate would descend and snatch us apart just as we had achieved freedom and happiness.' She wrote fiercely to Violet in January 1907: 'If either you or Kitty ever speak of my marriage again I shall write you such a lecture upon the carnal sins as will make you fall into each others arms' . Clive Bell (considered by Thoby a mixture between Shelley and a country squire) first proposed to her sister Vanessa in August 1905, and again in July 1906. Vanessa wrote to her artist friend Margery Snowdon on 13th August 1905: 'I could no more marry him than I could fly – so there's an end of it'. However, a cataclysmic event was about to precipitate her acceptance of this unlikely suitor, thus bringing Virginia's fears into reality.

Having sold a piece of writing by Thackeray to pay for his Bar fees (he was to become a barrister), the remaining funds were used by Thoby for a family holiday to Greece. It was also an opportunity for Vanessa to distance herself from Clive. Thoby and Adrian set off first and the sisters, accompanied by Violet Dickinson, departed shortly afterwards on 8th September 1906, meeting their brothers at Olympia. They visited Corinth, Athens, Nauplia and Mycenae, but Vanessa fell ill with appendicitis and the trip was abandoned. When they arrived back in London on 1st November, they found Thoby (who had gone on ahead) also dangerously ill with typhoid fever. Over the course of the following month, Virginia was a stoic nurse to her siblings, organising doctors, nurses and the house with very few complaints. Slowly Vanessa recovered, but Thoby did not. He died of an operation to treat an ulcer associated with typhoid fever on 20th November 1906. On 22nd November, Vanessa accepted Clive Bell's proposal of marriage. Virginia was thus plunged into a second loss: her beloved brother was gone and her sister was to be taken in marriage. To add insult to injury, both she and Adrian were asked to leave 46 Gordon Square by the time the Bells' honeymoon was over. It seemed that the brief period of freedom and happiness was at an end.

In her memoir 'A Sketch of the Past', she recalled making a pact with Adrian 'that we would go on talking about [Thoby], "for there are so many dead people now"'; and two years later she wrote to Madge Vaughan: 'I feel immensely old, and as though the best in us had gone.' In fact, after Thoby died, she continued to keep him alive in letters to Violet Dickinson who was also dangerously ill with typhoid and who was considered too weak to survive the news. Five days after his death she wrote to Violet: 'Thoby is going on splendidly. He is very cross with his nurses, because they wont give him mutton chops and beer; and he asks why he cant go for a ride with Bell, and look for wild geese. Then nurse says "wont tame ones do" at which we laugh.' It was only when she read a review of Frederick Maitland's *Life and Letters of Sir Leslie Stephen*, which mentioned that the book had appeared on the day of Thoby's death, that Violet was disabused. Her brother went on to haunt the pages of Virginia's subsequent fictional writing, he is Jacob Flanders of *Jacob's Room*, Percival of *The Waves* (which she considered dedicating to him), and there are elements of him in many other minor characters.

This sorrow was compounded by the obvious happiness felt by Vanessa who was characterised by Virginia in her letters at this time as 'divinely happy', 'a beautiful wise child', sitting 'hung with variegated gems, by a large vase of roses, and a fire of hot coals. She [...] exhales a great bounteous atmosphere – the essence of amethyst and amber.' However, she wrote melancholically to Violet in early January 1907: 'I realise that that is all over, and I shall never see her alone any more; and Clive is a new part of her, which I must learn to accept.' She wondered cruelly at Vanessa's choice: 'It does seem strange and intolerable sometimes. When I think of father and Thoby and then see that funny little creature twitching his pink skin and jerking out his little spasm of laughter I wonder what odd freak there is in

Nessa's eyesight.' After the engagement, Vanessa and Clive spent time at Clive's family home, Cleeve House, which Vanessa came to loathe for its upper middle class tastes and conservatism, a place where 'talk of diseases [was] the only variation on talk of the weather'.

Vanessa and Clive were eventually married on 7th February 1907. After the wedding the Bells went on honeymoon to Manorbier in Pembrokeshire and Virginia's letters to her new brother-in-law demanded him to give intimate caresses to her sister as a reminder to him of her own rights to Vanessa's affection: 'give my love to my sister, and, if you like, kiss her left eye, with the eyelid smoothed over the curve, and just blue on the crest'.

While the Bells were away, Virginia and Adrian moved, at the end of March 1907, to 29 Fitzroy Square, not far from their sister, but far enough to feel isolated from her newfound happiness. They once again faced opposition from conservative friends and family as to their choice of location: 'Beatrice comes round, inarticulate with meaning, and begs me not to take the house because of the neighbourhood.' They slowly began to drop more and more of the old guard from their acquaintance, including the devoted Violet Dickinson and the Vaughans, who figured less and less in their social circle. Virginia and Adrian were not ideally suited as housemates; Adrian annoyed Virginia by being morose and childish, while he found her malicious and mocking. On the Bells' return, The Friday Club continued at 46 Gordon Square and in response Adrian and Virginia created their own evenings with a wider and more eclectic group including Sydney Waterlow, Henry Lamb, Charles Tennyson, Edward Hilton Young, Beatrice Thynne, Janet Case and Lady Ottoline Morrell.

At the same time as this avant-garde was being formed, Virginia continued to write reviews and also began her first novel while on holiday in 1908, which she provisionally entitled 'Melymbrosia'. Progress on this debut novel was slow, held up by illness, family duties and other writing commitments. She worried that the writing might be 'd–d', that it was 'a most agitating work – and probably a will o' the wisp'. These concerns materialised in dreams as she revealed to Clive Bell: 'I dreamt last night that I was showing father the manuscript of my novel; and he snorted, and dropped it on to a table, and I was very melancholy, and read it this morning, and thought it bad.' Using Clive as her first male sounding board, she confided the ambitious plans she had for revolutionising novel-writing: 'I shall re-form the novel and capture multitudes of things at present fugitive, enclose the whole, and shape infinite strange shapes.' In other letters to Madge Vaughan and Lady Robert Cecil (Nelly) she is similarly desirous to find her voice: 'how I wish I could write a novel!' she laments to Madge; 'Oh how I should like to – discover how to write!' she exclaims to Nelly. She was to rewrite 'Melymbrosia' at least eight times before its publication as *The Voyage Out* in 1915; a tortuous process, demonstrative of her perfectionism.

It was through this novel, combined with the birth of Julian Heward Bell (who demanded much of Vanessa's attention) and a visit to Cornwall with the Bells in April 1908, that she began an ill-judged flirtation with Clive, for which, according to other members of the group, Vanessa never forgave her. To Clive, in characteristic Lothario style, the 'affair' was to be 'no less and [...] not much more than a delightful little infidelity, ending up in bed', but Virginia, who had no intention of sleeping with Clive, saw it as a chance to show off her learning to a man whose attention she could steal from her beloved, but neglectful, sister.[15] She wrote to Violet, 'it will really be some time before I can separate him from her'. At the height of their intimacy at the beginning of 1909, a new game was devised. The letter writing game saw the circle of friends attempting to write a collaborative novel, by taking on the characters of made-up eighteenth-century style ladies and gentlemen. Virginia was Eleanor Hayding, Clive and Vanessa were James and Clarissa Philips, Lytton was Vane Hatherly, Saxon was Mr Ilchester, and

Philip and Ottoline Morrell were Sir Julius and Lady Caroline Eastnor (the Morrells were new friends who had created an artistic salon at their houses – Ottoline was often the victim of the group's ridicule). The game allowed the flirtation between Clive and Virginia to continue under the pretence of pretence and enabled Vanessa and Lytton to confront Virginia more openly about the liaison. The game was soon dropped and Clive, perceiving that their relationship would never be consummated, began various other affairs instead, the most significant and long-lasting of which was with Mary Hutchinson.

Later in 1909 Virginia accompanied Adrian and Saxon Sydney-Turner to the opera at Bayreuth where she felt out of place and was unable to enter into their almost religious passion for Wagner. She related to her sister that they had told her: 'I shant know anything about it until I have heard it [Parsifal] 4 times' and they made her 'read the libretto in German, which trouble[d] [her] a good deal'; she also lamented the state of the audience who were 'dowdy' and 'drab'. Only a few years later she began to wonder at her taste for Wagner: 'I will never go again […] My eyes are bruised, my ears dulled, my brain a mere pudding of pulp – O the noise and the heat, and the bawling sentimentality, which used once to carry me away, and now leaves me sitting perfectly still.' Her letters to Vanessa while away in Germany were deeply affectionate and she reflected increasingly on the future of her new nephew, Julian, who would, she imagined, come to desire 'eccentric relations' of whom she would be one: 'Can't you imagine how airily he would produce her, on Thursday nights,' she asked Vanessa and then envisaged what he would say to his friends: '"I have an Aunt who copulates in a tree, and thinks herself with child by a grasshopper – charming isn't it? She dresses in green, and my mother sends her nuts from the Stores."' This was a role that she went on to perform with relish for all of Vanessa's three children.

1910 was a hugely significant year both for Virginia and for the London art scene. In January, Virginia volunteered to assist the women's suffrage movement by addressing envelopes. It was the first time she had become a political activist and she used this experience as material for her second novel, *Night and Day* (1919), which would feature a NUWSS (National Union of Women's Suffrage Societies) office. This work was interrupted on 10th February by the infamous Dreadnought Hoax, though Virginia did claim afterwards that the prank was, like her work for women's suffrage, of national importance: 'I am glad to think that I too have been of help to my country,' she said in her talk on the Hoax many years later.[16] Orchestrated by Horace Cole, with whom Adrian had carried out a similar practical joke in Cambridge a few years before, and with the help of Anthony Buxton, Guy Ridley, Duncan Grant and Virginia (Duncan and Virginia stepped in at the last minute), the hoaxers disguised themselves as the Emperor of Abyssinia, his entourage, translator and Foreign Office official and requested a tour of one of the navy's newest and finest war ships, the *Dreadnought*. Little did they know that the Stephens' more conventional cousin, William Fisher, was Flag Commander and there were a number of tense moments when they feared they would be exposed. The hoax made the papers, which outraged the Fishers and the establishment and resulted in Duncan and Horace Cole being abducted and tapped on the behind as punishment. According to anecdote, Horace pointed out that the navy should take the cane as it was their own stupidity which had enabled the success of the prank; they allowed him to return the favour. However, within a few months of this practical joke, Virginia fell ill and was taken to a nursing home in Twickenham where she spent six weeks. Writing to her sister who was pregnant with her second son Quentin at the time, she was plaintive: 'I really dont think I can stand much more of this,' she wrote. She was on the road to recovery when her nephew Quentin was born on 19th August and she managed to resume her novel and a degree of social intercourse in the autumn, just in time to witness one of the most important events in the history of British art.

'In or about December, 1910, human character changed'; in this famous statement Virginia was indirectly referring to the First Post-Impressionist Exhibition (originally entitled 'Manet and the Post-Impressionists') organised by the energetic painter Roger Fry whom the Bells had met earlier that year. Virginia later recalled in 'Reminiscences':

> It must have been in 1910 I suppose that Clive one evening rushed upstairs in a state of the highest excitement. He had just had one of the most interesting conversations of his life. It was with Roger Fry. They had been discussing the theory of art for hours. He thought Roger Fry the most interesting person he had met since Cambridge days. So Roger appeared. He appeared, I seem to think, in a large ulster coat, every pocket of which was stuffed with a book, a paint box or something intriguing; special tips which he had bought from a little man in a back street; he had canvases under his arms; his hair flew; his eyes glowed.

The exhibition was inspired by Fry, Bell and MacCarthy's trip to Paris where they saw and selected paintings by Picasso, Matisse, Cézanne, Manet, Gauguin, Derain and van Gogh. Interestingly, though these painters were largely of the previous century and well-known on the continent, they were mostly unknown in London. The exhibition caused a massive stir when it opened at the Grafton Galleries on 8th November 1910. The paintings were castigated as the 'output of a lunatic asylum' by *The Pall Mall Gazette*; the *Morning Post* critic argued that 'Cézanne mistook his vocation; he should have been a butcher'; while the *Daily Telegraph* critic threw down his exhibition catalogue in disgust. It turned out to be great publicity and launched these artists onto the British art scene with aplomb. Virginia and Vanessa were inspired and excited by what they saw and responded to the exhibition both in paint and in words, though they also caused a stir themselves at the Post-Impressionist Ball by dressing up as Gauguin's South Sea beauties – they were barely decent. Vanessa recorded in an unpublished memoir, quoted in Francis Spalding's biography: 'It is impossible I think that any other single exhibition can ever have had so much effect as did that on the rising generation [...] here was a sudden pointing to a possible path, a sudden liberation and encouragement to feel for oneself which were absolutely overwhelming [...] it was as if one might say things one has always felt instead of trying to say things that other people told one to feel'.[17] The exhibition was repeated in 1912, only this time with home-grown talent, and which included paintings by both Vanessa and Duncan; this led to them contributing pieces to Roger's Omega Workshop (1913–19), which sold furniture, textiles and fashion produced by Post-Impressionist-inspired artists. Virginia was jealous: it seemed that the artists were far more advanced than the writers and she resolved to redress the balance. In a much later essay on the painter Walter Sickert, Virginia articulated the similarities between words and paint, an observation that was made possible by the Post-Impressionist exhibitions and her relationship with Vanessa, Roger, Clive and Duncan: 'It is a very complex business, the mixing and marrying of words that goes on, probably un-consciously, in the poet's mind to feed the reader's eye. All great writers are great colourists, just as they are musicians into the bargain; they always contrive to make their scenes glow and darken and change to the eye.'

Shortly after the first exhibition Vanessa, Clive, Roger and H.T.J. Norton went on holiday to Turkey where Vanessa had a miscarriage and a mental breakdown. Useless in dealing with illness, Clive left the care of his wife to Roger, with whom Vanessa subsequently fell in love. Virginia rushed across Europe to nurse her sister and to bring her back home, but Virginia's own problems with mental health were far from over and once her sister was out of danger she wrote worryingly to her: 'I could not write, and all the devils came out – hairy black ones. To be 29 and unmarried – to be a failure – childless – insane too, no writer.' Since her sister's wedding, Virginia felt increasing pressure from friends and family to marry; she courted and flirted with admirers (mainly to provide amusing gossip for her sister whose attention she was increasingly desperate to reclaim). There was a minor flirtation with Walter Headlam in 1906–7 and she overplayed a flirtation with Rupert Brooke in 1909. Proposals came in from Edward Hilton Young and Lytton Strachey in 1909, Sydney Waterlow and Walter Lamb in 1911 (Lamb was critical of Bloomsbury which he likened, quite rightly, to a 'hornet's nest'), but all came to nought. During this time Lytton Strachey was writing to Leonard Woolf in Ceylon with tales of Virginia's chastity and beauty; an unlikely cupid, Lytton's darts reached across the world and brought Leonard back from Ceylon in 1911 ostensibly to woo Virginia. He had met the Stephen sisters before and recorded his initial impressions of them in his autobiography: 'the observant observer would have noticed at the back of the two Miss Stephens' eyes a look which would have warned him to be cautious, a look which belied the demureness, a look of great intelligence, hypercritical, sarcastic, satirical'.[18] He would later base his novel *The Wise Virgins* (1914) on his impressions of the Stephen sisters and his courtship of Virginia in particular. However, undeterred by this rather terrifying initial impression, Leonard moved into the commune at 38 Brunswick Square. The house was taken in 1911 so that Virginia and Adrian could take their friends as lodgers, thus saving money and diluting the time the two of them spent together. Keynes, Duncan Grant and Leonard Woolf were selected as their tenants. Virginia risked social scandal as the only woman in the house, but it gave her the opportunity to speak to Leonard who she characterized as 'a penniless Jew'.

Virginia alternately loved and hated London. It was a caco-phonous muddle full of 'roar & rattle & confusion' with 'no bird noises, no sighings & moanings of trees & green growing things – no splash of water'; it was 'very much like Hell' and yet, she conceded, 'ones mind "grows mouldy in the country" – Here at any rate one has no excuse for a speck of rust', and that the city 'attracts, stimulates, gives me a play & a story & a poem, without any trouble'. The later 'Street Haunting: A London Adventure' (1927) and *The London Scene* essays written as a series for *Good Housekeeping* in the early 1930s explore the inspirational influence of the London streets on Virginia's writing. To counteract the intensity of London she took a country house, which she named Little Talland House after her childhood holiday home, but in 1912 Virginia gave up Little Talland House and she and Vanessa took on a five year lease of a country house, Asheham near Firle, where friends and family could go to avoid London. Leonard was invited for weekends. His first proposal to Virginia was on 11th January 1912 and, though rebuffed, he renewed his suit in further letters. On 1st May she explained to him: 'I will not look upon marriage as a profession [...] both of us want a marriage that is a tremendous living thing, always alive, always hot, not dead and easy in parts as most marriages are.' Leonard took this rather cold letter as encouragement and resigned from his position in Ceylon in the hope that Virginia would reconsider her refusal – she did. He remembers the moment when she agreed to marry him in his autobiography: 'I had lunch with Virginia in her room and we sat talking afterwards, when suddenly Virginia told me that she loved me and would marry me [...] We both felt that in those 10 hours from after lunch to midnight when we got back to Brunswick Square we had seemed to drift through a beautiful, vivid dream'.[19] They were married at St Pancras Register Office on 10th August 1912, with only Vanessa and Clive Bell, George and Gerald Duckworth, Duncan Grant, Roger Fry, Saxon Sydney-Turner, Aunt Mary Fisher and Frederick Etchells in attendance. It was a quiet and informal ceremony, comically interrupted by Vanessa who enquired whether she might change her son Quentin's name.

This was to be a marriage of minds rather than of bodies. Virginia was excited about what they would do and achieve; she described them as having a 'bees-nest of plans and theories in our heads', but of sex she wrote to Leonard prior to accepting him: 'I feel no physical attraction in you. There are moments – when you kissed me the other day was one – when I feel no more than a rock.' In a letter to her friend Katherine Cox after their marriage she was puzzled: 'Why do you think people make such a fuss about marriage and copulation? Why do some of our friends change upon losing chastity? Possibly my great age makes it less of a catastrophe; but certainly I find the climax immensely exaggerated.' The couple consulted Vanessa about 'the goat's coldness' when they returned from their honeymoon. Vanessa responded unhelpfully, as she related in a letter to her husband: 'I think I perhaps annoyed her but may have consoled him by saying that I thought she never had understood or sympathised with sexual passion in men. Apparently she still gets no pleasure at all from the act, which I think is curious.' Nevertheless, Leonard and Virginia's letters show an enviable affection and mutual respect for one another; he is her mongoose, she his mandrill and they spent very little time apart during their thirty-eight-year marriage.

On their return from honeymoon they moved into Clifford's Inn. They had both finished their first novels; Leonard *The Village in the Jungle* (which was published by Edward Arnold in 1913), and Virginia *The Voyage Out* (which was to be published by her half-brother Gerald's publishing house, Duckworth, in 1915). Leonard was also writing *The Wise Virgins,* which he had started on their honeymoon. 'Leonard is in the middle of a new novel;' Virginia wrote to Violet, 'but as the clock strikes twelve, he begins an article upon Labour for some pale sheet, or a review of French literature for the Times, or a history of Co-operation.' His work ethic was impressive. He was also attending various political conferences on women's co-operatives and the Russian Revolution; he was secretary of the Labour Party's Advisory Committee on International Questions and writing a series of political papers and books, including *International Government*

(1916), *The Future of Constantinople* (1917) and *Cooperation and the Future of Industry* (1918). He came to the notice of the Fabians Sydney and Beatrice Webb in 1913 for his political work with the Northern Guilds, and through them began to work for the *New Statesman* and then later in 1919 became the editor of *The International Review*. Virginia admired and respected his dedication. Their sympathies and interests aligned and their happiness seemed assured, but sadly her prediction of 1905 that her mental breakdown was 'now fairly put away' and she 'need think no more of it' was soon to be proven wrong. From 1913 to 1915, she struggled with bouts of severe depression followed by moments of mania during which she babbled continuously and became violent (particularly towards Leonard). On 9th September 1913 she attempted suicide by taking one hundred grains of veronal (a barbiturate used to aid sleep). After incarceration in a rest home, she gradually stabilised, writing plaintive letters to Leonard and Vanessa, full of affection, guilt and promises of reform, but this breakdown was followed by another in 1915 during which she became incoherent and lapsed into a coma. It was a slow and painful process of recovery; she gradually put on weight, her mind became calmer, her letters more coherent and light-hearted. To Vanessa she wrote: 'I feel my brains, like a pear, to see if its ripe; it will be exquisite by September.' Leonard's autobiography is particularly detailed about this period of mental illness and Virginia herself tried to articulate the feeling in her diary many years later: 'Oh its beginning its coming – the horror – physically like a painful wave swelling about the heart – tossing me up.' She also wrote out some of the pain of this period in her 1925 novel *Mrs Dalloway* in which Septimus Warren Smith, suffering from shell-shock and besieged by dictatorial doctors, commits suicide.

The First World War, which sends the fictional character of Septimus mad, barely features in Virginia's letters and diaries, yet it had a massive impact on Bloomsbury, dispersing it, refocusing it, reframing it. In March 1916, for example, Virginia wrote to Katherine Cox: 'Bloomsbury is vanished like the morning mist.'

Many of the group were conscientious objectors. Vanessa and Virginia campaigned on behalf of their friends and family for exemption from service; Clive wrote against it in a controversial pamphlet entitled *Peace at Once* (spring 1915) published by the National Labour Party Press; Leonard was exempt due to the tremor in his hand and Virginia's mental instability; Lytton Strachey was also exempt for being too delicate to fight; Duncan Grant and his then lover David Garnett were put to work on the land fruit picking at Wissett, then at Charleston near Firle, to which they moved in 1916 and where Duncan and Vanessa continued to live for the rest of their lives. 'The war at anyrate has done some funny things among our friends,' Virginia wrote to Molly MacCarthy in 1916 while thinking of Clive as a farm labourer at Garsington. Virginia herself was clear that 'patriotism is a base emotion' and later went on to attack all war and warmongering in her more strident feminist tract, *Three Guineas* (1938). John Maynard Keynes worked for the Treasury and, along with Leonard who wrote *International Government* (1916), later played a central role in forming the ill-fated, but well-intentioned, League of Nations. Keynes also wrote *The Economic Consequences of the Peace* (1919) in which he predicted the outbreak of the Second World War. On Armistice Day, like many of her friends, Virginia was melancholy and detached from the celebrations: 'I think the rejoicing, so far as I've seen it, has been very sordid and depressing.' To her it seemed that there was little worth celebrating about such a wasteful war.

Her first novel, *The Voyage Out*, appeared on 26th March 1915 at the height of the conflict, though Virginia was undergoing a rest cure for her mental illness at the time. It was well received. The story played upon the ignorance in which young women were kept and she took the opportunity to satirize a number of her friends and family including Clive and Vanessa Bell, Ottoline Morrell and Lytton Strachey. When she was well enough to appreciate the comments of friends she responded warmly.

To Lytton Strachey's praise that the novel was 'very, very un-victorian!'[20] she replied: 'Your praise is far the nicest of any I've had […] I suspect your criticism about the failure of conception is quite right […] What I wanted to do was to give the feeling of a vast tumult of life, as various and disorderly as possible, which should be cut short for a moment by the death, and go on again – and the whole was to have a sort of pattern, and be somehow controlled.' It was a plan that she was to put into action in her subsequent novels. While in the early stages of writing her third novel, *Jacob's Room*, in 1920 she re-read *The Voyage Out* with a more critical eye, perhaps to avoid its mistakes. She described it as 'a harlequinade' and 'an assortment of patches – here simple & severe – here frivolous & shallow – here like God's truth – here strong & free flowing as I could wish. What to make of it, Heaven knows. The failures are ghastly enough to make my cheeks burn.' At the same time that she was recovering, she began work on her second novel, an arguably more conventional piece eventually published as *Night and Day* in 1919. The idea began after a visit to see Vanessa, on whom she based the hero-ine, Katharine Hilbery. To Vanessa she wrote: 'I am very much interested in your life, which I think of writing another novel about. Its fatal staying with you – you start so many new ideas.'

Progress on *Night and Day* was interrupted by the purchase of a hand printing press in early 1917 with which the Woolfs established the Hogarth Press (named after Hogarth House, which they had leased from the summer of 1915). It was initially set up on the dining room table, Virginia sorting the type (an activity which doubled as a form of therapy) and Leonard work-ing the press. 'We get so absorbed,' she enthused to Vanessa on 26th April, 'we can't stop; I see that real printing will devour one's entire life.' Most importantly their own press meant 'writing anything one likes, and not for an Editor', it freed her of the judgements of others, a luxury that made her friend and fellow writer Katherine Mansfield particularly jealous. Their first publication was entitled *Two Stories* and contained Virginia's

'The Mark on the Wall' and Leonard's 'Three Jews' with wood-cuts by Dora Carrington (one of the younger generation known, rather unfairly, as the 'Bloomsbury bunnies' or 'cropheads' on account of their haircuts). It was published in July 1917 and quickly sold out. New arrivals on the Bloomsbury literary scene, Katherine Mansfield and T.S. Eliot, looked set to provide more material for them to publish. Virginia had met Katherine in February 1917 and had written that she 'stinks like a – well civet cat that had taken to street walking', though she also admitted on the same page that 'she is so intelligent & inscrutable that she repays friendship'. She met T.S. Eliot the following year in November 1918, describing him as 'a polished, cultivated, elaborate young American [...] very intellectual, intolerant, with strong views of his own, & a poetic creed'. In 1918 Katherine Mansfield's *Prelude* was published and they were offered James Joyce's *Ulysses* that spring, but the press was too small to take it and no professional printer would risk prosecution for obscenity by printing it. Virginia's *Kew Gardens* followed on 12th May 1919 and had to be reprinted after a positive review in the *TLS*. It appeared with their publication of T.S. Eliot's *Poems* and John Middleton Murry's *The Critic in Judgment*, though these were less well received at the time. The greatest success belonged to Lytton Strachey whose book, *Eminent Victorians*, published by Chatto and Windus not the Woolfs, was received with acclaim – Virginia was characteristically jealous. Nevertheless, over the course of their publishing career the Woolfs showed great foresight, publishing Mansfield, Eliot, Forster, Clive Bell, Fry and Hope Mirrlees as well as James Strachey's translation of the complete works of Freud as part of the Psychoanalytic Library. They also, after *Night and Day*, published all of Virginia's novels.

On Christmas Day 1918, Vanessa gave birth to her third and last child, the product of her relationship with the painter Duncan Grant. Duncan ended their physical relationship after the birth of his daughter, though both he and Vanessa remained close friends and artistic collaborators for the rest of their lives.

Virginia delighted in imagining the unborn child: 'I hope you'll bring the unborn baby up to appreciate me; I'm already half in love with her/him. It will have lovely great eyes; soft hair; a divine mouth; and then only think what a gifted lovable sprite it will be so understanding from its earliest years, and as wise as an idol, and as witty as a humming bird'; and after her birth she offered suitable names for the new baby: Clarissa, Miriam, Rachel, Venetia, Sabina, Clara, Sarah, Sara, Euphrosyne, Nerissa, Griselda, Lesley. Three months later the new arrival was named Angelica. Domestically, Virginia's letters in the 1910s are full of Vanessa's children, servant problems (scenes, resignations, reconciliations) and regular house hunting. In London there was Brunswick Square, Clifford's Inn, Hogarth and Suffield House in Richmond; and in the country there was Little Talland House, Asheham, the Round House in Lewes (bought and sold within a few weeks), cottages at Zennor and, most importantly, Monk's House. Hogarth House gave its name to the press, but it was Monk's House with which Virginia has come to be most closely associated. Situated in the village of Rodmell, four miles from Vanessa's house, Charleston, Monk's House provided the Woolfs with the perfect writers' retreat. They bought it on 1st July 1919 and Virginia wrote in her diary entry two days later: 'We own Monks House (this is almost the first time I've written a name which I hope to write many thousands of times before I've done with it) for ever.' G.E. Easdale in the 1930s described how the furniture in the house was painted by Vanessa and Duncan, how books and apples lay everywhere, how much Leonard loved the bountiful garden and how he was received there 'with such kindness'.[21] Leonard lived there until his death in 1969.

Back in London at the end of the 1910s, the Woolfs were at the heart of literary life in Bloomsbury, though still living in Richmond. Buying Hogarth House and its neighbour Suffield House was a way to avoid 'being swept into the vortex' of Bloomsbury where her sister, brother and the Stracheys lived. The Woolfs were reading, writing and publishing their own and others' work, so when *Night and Day* appeared on 20th October 1919, some were disappointed by this more conventional romantic comedy exploring the break with Victorianism. Kitty Maxse and Jake Hutchinson thought it dull; E.M. Forster was disappointed by it; Katherine Mansfield despised it. Mansfield claimed in her review for *The Athenaeum* on 21st November 1919 that: 'it makes us feel old and chill: we had never thought to look upon its like again'.[22] But it had served a useful function, as Woolf revealed many years later: 'it taught me a great deal, or so I hoped, like a minute Academy drawing: what to leave out: by putting it all in'. Other critics and friends were more positive. J.T. Sheppard and Ka Cox liked it; Dr Savage considered it 'one of the great novels of the world', and the book opened the door to society hostess Sybil Colefax, which led Virginia to conclude to Roger that 'the praise if anything worse than the blame'. She dedicated the book to her sister who had inspired it: 'To Vanessa Bell but, looking for a phrase I found none to stand beside your name.'

But even as she was receiving this praise and blame Virginia had already moved on, the germ of an idea had begun for her next novel which proved to be a radical departure from the more linear narratives of *The Voyage Out* and *Night and Day*. In her diary she recorded that in her next piece there should be 'no scaffolding; scarcely a brick to be seen; all crepuscular'. She continued: 'conceive mark on the wall, K[ew]. G[ardens]. & unwritten novel taking hands & dancing in unity. What the unity shall be I have yet to discover: the theme is blank to me; but I see immense possibilities in the form I hit upon more or less by chance 2 weeks ago'. Thus at the end of 1919 she found herself married, a publisher, with two novels under her belt and another, more experimental work, in embryo. No wonder she wrote so cheerfully on the 28 December 1919 of herself and Leonard: 'I daresay we're the happiest couple in England.'

The 1920s

On 21st May 1922, Virginia described her place in the literary canon to her old Greek teacher Janet Case: 'But don't you agree with me that the Edwardians, from 1895 to 1914, made a pretty poor show. By the Edwardians, I mean Shaw, Wells, Galsworthy, the Webbs, Arnold Bennett. We Georgians have our work cut out for us, you see. […] Orphans is what I say we are – we Georgians' . To Virginia her predecessors were on the wrong literary track, particularly in their efforts with the novel. Though her first two novels were largely well, if not enthusiastically, received and were being published by Doran in the United States, they were still in many senses linked to the Edwardian traditions of linear plot and realist characterisation. However, with the short stories 'The Mark on the Wall' (1917) and 'Kew Gardens' (1919) she had made some progress towards experimenting with narrative perspective and style, and stated in a letter to the painter Jacques Raverat in 1922 that she was 'thinking, thinking, thinking about literature'. She pondered in her diary halfway through the decade how best to describe what she intended to produce: 'I have an idea that I will invent a new name for my books to supplant "novel". A new – by Virginia Woolf. But what?' Though she had no name for her projected work, it was to be a new form, a complete break from the Edwardian tradition. In March 1921 the Hogarth Press published a collection of Virginia's short stories entitled *Monday or Tuesday*; it included

'A Haunted House', 'A Society', 'Monday or Tuesday', 'An Unwritten Novel', 'The String Quartet', 'Blue & Green', 'Kew Gardens' and 'The Mark on the Wall'. With characteristic pessimism she imagined lukewarm reviews from *The Times* and sarcasm from the *Westminster Gazette* and *Pall Mall Gazette*, but was relieved with praise from her sister and from Lytton Strachey, whom Virginia considered 'the choicest of us'. This volume of experimental stories also marked her lifelong alliance with Harcourt Brace, which took over from Doran as her American publishers. When this collection appeared, Virginia was in the midst of writing her third novel, *Jacob's Room* (1922).

At the beginning of the decade it seemed to Virginia that Bloomsbury society was diversified thanks to the war, but not sanitised. It was a 'rabbit warren', but it still seethed with gossip and indiscretions. Bloomsbury's original 'members' were involved in a variety of intrigues. There were Clive's various love affairs which became increasingly ridiculous; Lytton's *ménage à trois* at Tidmarsh with Ralph Partridge and Dora Carrington (Lytton loved Ralph, who loved Carrington, who loved Lytton); Keynes's affair with the Russian ballerina Lydia Lopokova, whom Virginia and Vanessa considered beneath him; Vanessa's liaison with Duncan and the concealment of his being Angelica's father; Duncan's liaisons with a string of male lovers. Vanessa's household, Virginia felt, was at the centre of Bloomsbury; she characterized it as a Shakespearean comedy and an 'astonishing brightness in the heart of darkness. Julian coming in with his French lesson; Angelica hung with beads, riding on Roger's foot; Clive claret coloured & yellow like a canary; Duncan vague in the background, sitting astride a chair'. Everyone was working hard. Clive was writing *Since Cézanne* (1922) and drafting *Civilization* (1928); Vanessa was painting and mothering (she was described as the 'best of our women painters' by May John Alton in the *Nation* on 5th May 1923); Duncan's one-man show at the Paterson & Carfax Gallery in February 1920 was a success; Lytton published *Queen Victoria* (1921), which he dedicated to

Virginia and which she found to be 'not at all a meditative or profound book' (she was even more scathing of his later work *Elizabeth and Essex* (1928)); Keynes was working on a variety of economic papers; Adrian and his wife Karin were studying psychoanalysis with Dr James Glover; Molly MacCarthy started the Memoir Club (Virginia wrote '22 Hyde Park Gate', 'Old Bloomsbury' and 'Am I Snob' for it); Roger Fry had just published *Vision and Design* (1920); Forster was working in India (following which he published *A Passage to India* (1924)). Meanwhile, Leonard was embarking on a political career, and in May 1920 became the Labour candidate for the Combined English Universities, about which Virginia wrote to Violet Dickinson: 'Thank goodness, he's got no chance of getting in.' She supported him by going to Manchester to canvass for votes in March 1921, though she admitted to the astonished Mancunians that she would rather see the zoo than play the dutiful political wife. He and Virginia had also found the time to teach themselves enough Russian to assist S.T. Koteliansky with his translations of Dostoyevsky, Chekhov and Gorky. Throughout all of this Leonard was also managing the Hogarth Press, as well as the mental health of his wife.

It was against this backdrop of gossip, scandal, art, literature and politics that Virginia began writing *Jacob's Room*. It was to be an experiment in character, plot, structure and narrative style. Before beginning the novel, Virginia jotted down some thoughts both in her notebook and her diary:

> Suppose one thing should open out of another – as in An Unwritten Novel – only not for 10 pages but 200 or so – doesn't that give the looseness & lightness I want: doesn't that get closer & yet keep form & speed, & enclose every-thing, everything? [...] but the heart, the passion, humour, everything as bright as fire in the mist.

However, she worried that she might not be able to 'enclose the human heart' and that 'the damned egotistical self; which ruins

Joyce & Richardson' might creep in. As with all of her early novels, writing was difficult and sporadic: some days she recorded 'writing easily' and 'with great pleasure', others she would sit 'scratching out, putting in, scratching out', or would find herself at a 'full stop'. She was in a delicate mental state in June, July and August of 1921 and in her diary she recorded on 8th August:

> These, this morning, the first words I have written – to call writing – for 60 days; & those days spent in wearisome headache, jumping pulse, aching back, frets, fidgets, lying awake, sleeping draughts, sedatives, digitalis, going for a little walk, & plunging back into bed again – all the horrors of the dark cupboard of illness once more displayed for my diversion.

Similar bouts struck early in the following year when she turned forty, after which she wrote to Forster: 'Writing is still like heaving bricks over a wall'. She had three teeth removed in May 1922 in the hope that this might help to relieve her bouts of influenza and heart murmurs, which the doctors had informed Leonard might kill her in the near future. Though plagued with illness and self-doubt she was still chipping away at her novel.

Jacob's Room was based around the 'hero', Jacob Flanders, who was modelled on her brother Thoby; indeed, the book was a sort of elegy for him. This hero is particularly interesting because the reader is very rarely permitted to enter his mind and so his character is largely built up from the observations of all the other characters and narrator. In *Jacob's Room*, Virginia examined a number of interesting themes. Perhaps the most unusual of these was the unknowability of people; even the omniscient narrator does not know Jacob properly. 'It seems,' the narrator states, 'that a profound, impartial, and absolutely just opinion of our fellow-creatures is utterly unknown.' The novel also obliquely criticises the arrogance and jingoism of the patriarchal society which caused a generation of young men to die in the First World War. The narrator, in describing the futures of the young men at Cambridge, stops herself for 'there is no need to think of them grown old'. Jacob Flanders is one of these young men who is sent to war, but unlike the hero he is meant to be, he dies the same death as thousands of others. All that is left of him at the end of the novel is, poignantly, an empty room and a pair of shoes.

Prior to publication Virginia claimed: 'I have found out how to begin (at 40) to say something in my own voice'. This novel in her own voice was published on 27th October 1922 and was the first full-length novel published by the Hogarth Press. The publication of *Jacob's Room* under Virginia's own imprint meant freedom from her half-brother's publishing house. It also meant that her sister could design the cover and so continued an artistic liaison between them which would last for Virginia's lifetime. Vanessa's dust jackets also helped to create an in-house style, vital for the marketing of Hogarth's future publications. As usual Virginia worried about criticism, despite all of her declarations to the contrary. In August 1922, prior to publication, she fretted to Roger Fry: 'it is too much of an experiment to be a success' and to her diary confided: 'The thing now reads thin & pointless; the words scarcely dint the paper; & I expect to be told that I've written a graceful fantasy, without much bearing on real life.'

After publication the novel was praised by all of her close friends. She responded humbly to any criticisms they raised: Lytton suspected her of Romanticism; David Garnett felt she had failed with Realism; Leonard thought that she had 'no philosophy of life' and that her characters were 'ghosts [...] puppets, moved hither & thither by fate'. *Jacob's Room* also introduced her to the Sapphist, aristocrat and writer Vita Sackville-West who had read and admired the novel. Vita wrote to Virginia praising the novel and requesting an audience which was granted in December 1922, after which they entered into a lasting friendship punctuated by a short-lived love affair.

It seems that many reviewers did not know what to make of the novel. The reviewer for *The New Age* stated that 'the little flurries of prose poetry do not make art of this rag-bag of impressions',[23] while *The Yorkshire Post* was ambivalent: '*Jacob's Room* has no narrative, no design, above all, no perspective: [...] flickering, impermanent. Nevertheless, [...] she is, unlike most of her contemporaries, a genuine artist.'[24] Arnold Bennett in his article 'Is the Novel Decaying?' for *Cassell's Weekly* on 28th March 1923 argued: 'the characters do not vitally survive in the mind because the author has been obsessed by details of originality and cleverness.'[25] It was this article that provoked Virginia to write the essay 'Mr Bennett and Mrs Brown' which appeared in the *Nation and Athenaeum* on 1st December 1923 (it was revised as a lecture to the Society of Cambridge Heretics entitled 'Character in Fiction', given in May 1924). The article outlined and satirized the problems with Bennett, Wells and Galsworthy's style of characterisation, claiming that they never manage to represent the character of the imaginary Mrs Brown because they deal with everything surrounding her and connected to her, but fail to catch her essence. Virginia asked these Edwardian authors 'How shall I begin to describe this woman's character?' and imagined their response:

'Begin by saying that her father kept a shop in Harrogate. Ascertain the rent. Ascertain the wages of shop assistants in the year 1878. Discover what her mother died of. Describe cancer. Describe calico. Describe –' But I cried: 'Stop! Stop!' And I regret to say that I threw that ugly, that clumsy, that incongruous tool out of the window, for I knew that if I began describing the cancer and the calico, my Mrs Brown, that vision to which I cling though I know no way of imparting it to you, would have been dulled and tarnished and vanished for ever.

It was not an easy task to express on paper the life of a human being, which she described famously in her essay 'Modern

Fiction' (1925; originally published as 'Modern Novels' in the *TLS* in 1919) thus: 'Life is not a series of gig-lamps symmetrically arranged; life is a luminous halo, a semi-transparent envelope surrounding us from the beginning of consciousness to the end.' The difficulty was how to express this amorphous, ephemeral halo on paper without resorting to 'cancer and calico'. Thus, Virginia began her life's mission, not only of reinventing the style and shape of the novel, but the even more arduous task of representing psychologically realistic characters. Though she disclaimed *Jacob's Room* repeatedly as an 'experiment' and saw its flaws, thanks to this novel and her essays about the future of fiction, she was 'buoyed up [...] by the thought that I'm now, at last, going to bring it off – next time'.

Following the success of *Jacob's Room*, which reached a small, but select readership, the pressure of other responsibilities began to get in the way of her fiction. Requests for articles and reviews flooded in and she lamented to Gerald Brenan the amount of journalism she and her husband had undertaken:

> Here we are with our noses to the grindstone. The grind-stone is made of innumerable books which have to be tran-substantiated into precisely the right number of articles, containing the right sentiments, views and facts, in the right number of words at the right moment. [...] till all our precious time is over, and life, which surely has other uses, has poured in cataracts of printers ink, down the main gutter to the Thames.

She exclaimed privately: 'Oh the servants! Oh reviewing! Oh the weather!' Indeed, the servant problem was one of the central distractions of the 1920s. Lottie Hope, Nellie Boxall and their 'hysterics' were the subject of numerous letters and diary entries, but her response to them revealed as much about her own class politics as their ability to irritate: 'I am sick of the timid spiteful servant mind,' she moaned to her diary. These two live-in servants eventually left in 1924 and 1934 respectively. Such professional and domestic distractions were compounded by intermittent mental health problems, the beginnings of which were usually signalled by a headache and resulted in weeks and sometimes months in bed, seeing no one and writing little. She began to use her diary to 'writ[e] off the fidgets' which, she speculated in October 1920, were caused by 'having no children, living away from friends [in Richmond, where she lived until 1924], failing to write well, spending too much on food, growing old', but were also brought on by too much society, too much writing and jealousy of her sister's lifestyle. On 2nd January 1923 she confessed: 'I am in one of my moods [...] And what is it & why? A desire for children, I suppose; for Nessa's life' . Vanessa was still strong, stable and central, though they remained rivals and spent less time in each other's company during the 1920s as Vanessa began to disappear abroad in order to paint (she shared a villa at Cassis in southern France with Duncan). Virginia, 'susceptible to the faintest chord of dissonance' between them, recorded an argument in February 1922 concerning which of them lived the more extraordinary life. Virginia dwelt on her sister's intimations that she was 'settled & unadventurous' and felt 'discontent' after the exchange, reflecting in her diary that her 'life, I suppose, did not vigorously rush in' when her sister left the room. She confessed to Vanessa in a letter just over two weeks later: 'Yes, I was rather depressed when you saw me – What it comes to is this: you say "I do think you lead a dull respectable absurd life – lots of money, no children, everything so settled: and conventional. Look at me now – only sixpence a year – lovers – Paris – life – love – art – excitement – God! I must be off". This leaves me in tears.'

The Hogarth Press also began to encroach on her time in this decade. On 18th July 1920 she lamented to Ottoline Morrell: 'I'm afraid we must spend next Sunday as we are spending this – hot and cross, – almost hoping that there won't be any more orders tomorrow'; and yet in October 1921 they invested in a larger press (this was later given to Vita Sackville-West in 1930). They still had longer books printed by a professional printer, but smaller works were done by hand on their printing press at home; Eliot's *The Waste Land*, for example, was typeset by Virginia and hand-printed at the Hogarth Press in 1923. 'The Press is in the dining room, in the larder, and soon will be in bed with us,' she laughingly wrote to Violet Dickinson and admitted that it was 'clearly too lively & lusty to be carried on in this private way any longer.' In order to cope with the increasing volume of work, they entered into a series of unhappy alliances with young men who wanted to try their hands at the publishing business: Ralph Partridge, George H.W. Rylands and Angus Davidson among them. Leonard and Ralph had a particularly tumultuous relationship in the early 1920s. Leonard was stern and exacting, Ralph young and bullish. After one disagreement Virginia wrote sharply to Ralph: 'if you're going to tell me that you care more about it [the Hogarth Press] than I do, or know better what's good for it, I must reply that you're a donkey.' Ralph left the Hogarth Press on 14th March 1923, ostensibly to set up a rival press at Ham Spray with the patronage of Lytton Strachey. In the same year, Virginia met George Rylands. Known affectionately as 'Dadie', he voiced an interest in joining the press as a partner while writing his fellowship dissertation for Cambridge and began working for the Woolfs in July 1924, though he left in December to become a Fellow of King's College, Cambridge. Virginia was much more friendly with Dadie than with any of her other employees. She wrote of him: 'I feel considerable affection – so sensitive & tender is he' and they published two volumes of his poetry, as well as his fellowship dissertation. Dadie was replaced by Angus Davidson, with whom tensions, as with Ralph, mounted. There were petty arguments, which Virginia recorded in her diary:

I asked the time in the Press a week ago.
'Leonard can tell you' said Angus very huffily.

'Ask Angus. I don't seem to know' said Leonard very grumpy. And I saw Mrs C. lower her head over her typing & laugh. This was the tail of a terrific quarrel about the time between them. Angus was dismissed; but tells Nessa he wants to stay, could tempers be made compatible.

They could not, and Angus was replaced by a young apprentice, Richard Kennedy, in April 1928. Nevertheless, despite all of the hard work and vexations that the Hogarth Press evoked, Virginia did recognise in September 1925 that she was 'the only woman in England free to write what I like. The others must be thinking of series & editors.'

The press gave her a steady stream of new manuscripts to read, but she was also reading a number of influential authors who affected her own writing. In August 1922, she gave herself a writing prescription which she tried to adhere to: 'The way to rock oneself back into writing is this. First gentle exercise in the air. Second the reading of good literature. It is a mistake to think that literature can be produced from the raw.' Reading was clearly vital to her writing. She was particularly impressed with the work of Marcel Proust whom she first picked up in 1922; to Roger Fry she enthused:

Proust so titillates my own desire for expression that I can hardly set out the sentence. Oh if I could only write like that! I cry. And at the moment such is the astonishing vibration and saturation and intensification that he procures – theres something sexual in it – that I feel I can write like that, and seize my pen and then I *can't* write like that. Scarcely anyone so stimulates the nerves of language in me: it becomes an obsession.

She was less enthusiastic about the work of James Joyce, whose *Ulysses* the Hogarth Press had declined to publish on grounds of size, and the external printers on grounds of obscenity. Virginia was unimpressed in 1922; she was 'amused, stimulated, charmed interested' by it at first, but became 'puzzled, bored, irritated, & disillusioned as by a queasy undergraduate scratching his pimples'. To her mind, it was the 'illiterate, underbred book [...] of a self taught working man' who was 'egotistic, insistent, raw, striking, & ultimately nauseating', Nevertheless, she felt threatened enough by *Ulysses* to worry during the writing of *Jacob's Room* that what she was 'doing is probably being better done by Mr Joyce'. The other literary rival that she treated with similar caution was Katherine Mansfield who was achieving fame with her short stories (one of which the Hogarth Press had published). Virginia disliked what she perceived to be Mansfield's commonness, but recognised that Mansfield had a gift which rivalled her own; it caused a certain degree of jealousy between the two women. Virginia wrote to Roger Fry on 1st August 1920: 'Have you at all come round to her stories? I suppose I'm too jealous to wish you to, [...] I think the only thing is to confess it.' In May 1920, Virginia noted Katherine's 'fierce[ness]' about her art and 'a common certain understanding' between them; she was someone who Virginia could 'talk straight out to' and together they made 'a public of two'. She reflected that she felt 'the queerest sense of echo coming back to me from [Katherine's] mind'. Katherine was only in England intermittently while Virginia knew her, as she was suffering from tuberculosis, which eventually killed her on 9th January 1923 at a hospice in Fontainebleau, France. After she died Virginia felt depressed: 'When I began to write, it seemed to me there was no point in writing. Katherine wont read it. Katherine's my rival no longer.'

Uneasy relationships with critics also began to develop. John Middleton Murry (the husband of Katherine Mansfield) and Wyndham Lewis were both eager to knock the 'Bloomsberries' down to size. Of the latter she noted in a letter to Sydney Waterlow on 3rd May 1921: 'Wyndham Lewis has been abusing everyone I'm told, in his paper, and Roger and Nessa read him in shops, and won't buy him – which, as I say, proves that they fear him.' Referring to Lewis and Henry Tonks, she asked Clive Bell, 'What scurvy of the soul are they afflicted with that they must scratch in public?' and she spent hours discussing Murry's short-comings with her relatively new friend, T.S. Eliot, in June 1921. Of Murry's writing she was disparaging to Ottoline Morrell: 'I've just dropped The Things We Are, half paralysed with disgust and boredom[.] If Murry lives next door to you, I assure you the mildew will sprout in every room', while she claimed to Roger 'all one hopes is that he may bite each one of us in turn before he is finally discredited and shuffled off to some 10th rate Parisian Café, where you'll find him, 20 years hence, laying down the law to the illegitimate children of Alaister Crawley, Wyndham Lewis, and James Joyce.' However, the most import-ant (and strangely inspiring) of these uneasy relations with her critics was with Arnold Bennett. Bennett's criticism of her characterisation in *Jacob's Room* provoked the essay 'Mr Bennett and Mrs Brown', but it also encouraged a reassessment of her method when it came to her next novel, *Mrs Dalloway* (1925).

The seeds of *Mrs Dalloway* had been planted in *The Voyage Out*, where the Dalloways had already appeared as characters, as well as in her short story 'Mrs Dalloway in Bond Street' (1923). In this novel she developed a 'tunnelling process' to counteract the criticism of her characterisation by Leonard and Bennett, and through this she was able to 'tell the past by instalments'.'I dig out beautiful caves behind my characters,' she revealed, 'I think that gives exactly what I want; humanity, humour, depth. The idea is that the caves shall connect, & each comes to daylight at the present moment'. As with all of her previous novels the characters in *Mrs Dalloway* had their roots in real people: Mrs Dalloway herself was based on Kitty Maxse, with whom Virginia and Vanessa had been familiar in their Hyde Park Gate youth; while Madge Vaughan became Sally Seton; and Lydia Lopokova (who married Keynes in 1925) inspired Rezia Warren Smith. Kitty and Virginia had drifted apart after the Stephens had moved to Bloomsbury because Kitty did not approve of the way in which the siblings conducted their lives after their father's death. Virginia wrote to Margaret Llewelyn Davies in January 1920:

> I used to hate her friends and her views [...] We always did quarrel about what constitutes 'blood' and 'narrowness' – In fact, we parted, when I went to Fitzroy Sqre, on those grounds – so did Nessa [...] How she used to implore Nessa and me not to know people like Leonard!

However, by the time she was writing *Mrs Dalloway* (initially entitled 'The Hours'), Kitty was dead; it was thought to be suicide.

Virginia noted after Kitty's funeral in October 1922: 'Mrs Dalloway has branched into a book; & I adumbrate here a study of insanity & suicide: the world seen by the sane & the insane side by side – something like that. Septimus Smith? – is that a good name? – & to be more close to the fact than Jacob: but I think Jacob was a necessary step, for me, in working free.' It was difficult to tackle the sensitive subject of madness in her fiction, particularly as she drew heavily on her own experiences. To her diary she confided in June 1923: 'the mad part tries me so much, makes my mind squint so badly that I can hardly face spending the next weeks at it.' The novel's action takes place within a single day and sees Mrs Dalloway organising a party against which is set the mental breakdown and suicide of a shell-shocked ex-soldier, Septimus Warren Smith. As well as madness, the novel contains a veiled attack on the class system ('I want to criticise the social system, & to show it at work, at its most intense'); and her concerns that female identity was still seen as an adjunct to male identity.

There were the usual fears; Virginia was particularly worried in October 1923 that Clarissa's character 'may be too stiff, too glittering & tinsely'. She also found the revision process in early 1925 'the dullest part of the whole business'. However, she was pleased with Jacques Raverat's praise shortly before his death in March 1925; he had written, using his wife as amanuensis: 'Almost it's enough to make me want to live a little longer, to continue to receive such letters and such books.'[26] When the novel was published on 14th May 1925, it was received warmly, though unfavourable reviews in the *Western Mail*, *Scotsman* and *Calendar* upset her. Friends and family were largely impressed; Raymond Mortimer and E.M. Forster liked it, though Lytton thought there was 'a discordancy between the ornament (extremely beautiful) & what happens (rather ordinary – or unimportant)' which he blamed on Mrs Dalloway, but conceded, 'What can one call it but genius?' However, the completion and publication of *Mrs Dalloway* caused Virginia's mental issues to resurface and in August 1925 she fainted at Quentin's fifteenth birthday party fireworks, after which she resolved never to be 'unseated by the shying of that undependable brute, life, hag ridden as she is by my own queer, difficult nervous system.' The following year she studied her mental state. It formed a sort of self-analysis; entries on 31st July and 15th September 1926 entitled 'My own Brain' and 'A State of Mind' are particularly revealing. To cure it she prescribed: 'first, incessant brain activity; reading, & planning; second, a methodical system of inviting people here [...]; third, increased mobility'. She even wrote a light-hearted essay entitled 'On Being Ill', which was published in *The Criterion* in 1926.

At the same time as she was penning *Mrs Dalloway*, she was also amassing critical essays for *The Common Reader* (the working title was 'Reading'), which appeared a few weeks before *Mrs Dalloway* on 23rd April 1925. It was a testimony to all her years of diligent reading and reviewing and cemented her reputation as a virtuosic literary critic. Lytton, whose opinion she prized, thought the volume of essays superior to *Mrs Dalloway*, calling it 'divine, a classic' and public reviews were positive in the *TLS* (for which she had written since 1905), *The Manchester Guardian* and *The Observer*. Thus, by the mid-1920s, Virginia was the proud author of four novels, a plethora of reviews, a volume of serious criticism, and was joint owner of one of the most avant-garde publishing houses of the day.

Virginia had already started to plan her next novel before *Mrs Dalloway* was complete. She had envisaged her father as a subject for a short story as early as 17th October 1924 and 6th January 1925, and by 14th May 1925 she had formed a fuller plan: 'to have father's character done complete in it; & mothers; & St Ives; & childhood; & all the usual things I try to put in – life, death &c.' The book is split into three sections: the first sees the Ramsay family enjoying a holiday with their guests; the central section is shorter and shows the empty house being cleaned – it also reveals, through a series of asides, what has happened to the characters since that holiday; the final part sees the family returning, the youngest son's first trip to the lighthouse and the completion of the artist's painting started in the first section. In a later memoir Virginia recalled how the idea developed and hit her as she walked in London:

> Then one day walking round Tavistock Square I made up, as I sometimes make up my books, *To the Lighthouse*; in a great, apparently involuntary, rush. One thing burst into another. Blowing bubbles out of a pipe gives the feeling of the rapid crowd of ideas and scenes which blew out of my mind, so that my lips seemed syllabling of their own accord as I walked. What blew the bubbles? Why then? I have no notion. But I wrote the book very quickly.

It was a story about her childhood at St Ives (though set in Scotland) and concentrated particularly on the figures of her father and mother, who she claimed 'obsessed' her. It was also a story about Post-Impressionism and female independence. The figure of the female artist, Lily Briscoe, who was partly based on her sister, stands up to the opposition of men who say 'women can't write, women can't paint'. 'Never never have I written so easily, imagined so profusely' she enthused about the novel in

February 1926, but worried that the subject matter was too sentimental; that 'it may run too fast & free, & so be rather thin', and struggled with finding the right way to end on 5th September 1926. Nevertheless, it was 'subtler & more human' than her previous novels and towards the end of its composition in November 1926 she felt 'it is easily the best of my books, fuller than J[acob].'s R[oom], & less spasmodic, occupied with more interesting things than Mrs D[alloway]. & not complicated with all that desperate accompaniment of madness. It is freer & subtler I think'. It was finished on 14th January 1927, though the arduous process of rewriting was just beginning; she revised 'some parts 3 times over'.

Initial reactions from friends and family when it was published on 5th May 1927 were largely positive. She recorded that Leonard thought the novel a 'masterpiece' and a 'psychological poem'. Reviews were also positive, though she was disappointed by the rather tepid assessment of the *TLS* on 5th May 1927 in which the anonymous reviewer stated that the characters were 'not completely real' and 'lack something as individuals', while the central section was dismissed as 'not its strongest part'. However, when Vanessa read the novel, she realised how wedded to their shared childhood it was and wrote to Virginia with a mixture of pain and admiration:

> You have given me a portrait of mother which is more like her to me than anything I could ever have conceived possible. It is almost painful to have her so raised from the dead […] It was like meeting her again with oneself grown up and on equal terms it seems to me an astonishing feat of creation to have been able to see her in such a way […] So you see as far as portrait painting goes, you seem to me to be a supreme artist and it is so shattering to find oneself face to face with those two again that I can hardly consider anything else. In fact for the last two days I have hardly been able to attend to daily life.

The novel was therapeutic for both of them. Virginia claimed in her memoir that *To the Lighthouse* ceased her obsession with parents and her mother in particular: 'I no longer hear her voice; I do not see her,' she wrote, 'I suppose that I did for myself what psycho-analysts do for their patients. I expressed some very long felt and deeply felt emotion. And in expressing it I explained it and then laid it to rest.'

Shortly after its publication she lectured to Oxford women undergraduates on 'Poetry, Fiction and the Future', which was published afterwards as an article in the *New York Herald Tribune* on 14th August 1927. In this essay, which many contemporary critics take to be her fullest manifesto on writing, Virginia outlined the direction in which the novel needed to develop. 'It will be written in prose,' she claimed, 'but in prose which has many of the characteristics of poetry. It will have something of the exaltation of poetry, but much of the ordinariness of prose. It will be dramatic, and yet not a play.' She concluded in June 1927: 'I think, however, I am now almost an established figure – as a writer. They dont laugh at me any longer,' and indeed 'they' did not as she was awarded the Prix Femina on 2nd May 1928 for *To the Lighthouse*. As with all prizes and honours she was scathing of the ceremony: 'The prize was an affair of dull stupid horror: a function; not alarming; stupefying.' Nevertheless, she was now formally recognised as an author of standing.

Other excitements following the publication of *To the Lighthouse* included the solar eclipse for which she went to Yorkshire on 29th June 1927 with Vita and Harold Nicolson, Quentin, Leonard, Saxon and Ray Strachey. She had her hair shingled (it looked like a 'partridges rump', she wrote to Vanessa). They bought a second-hand Singer car on 15th July 1927. Later that month she went alone to stay with the American painters Ethel Sands and Nan Hudson at their Normandy chateau; and, much to her amusement, was pursued romantically by Ottoline Morrell's husband, Philip, who wrote her an ardent letter confessing his feelings. However, Philip was not the only person who fell for Virginia's charms in the 1920s.

When Virginia first met the lesbian aristocrat Vita Sackville-West (her married name was Nicolson, though she published under her maiden name) in December 1922, she was unimpressed: 'Not much to my severer taste – florid, moustached, parakeet coloured, with all the supple ease of the aristocracy, but not the wit of the artist. She writes 15 pages a day – has finished another book – publishes with Heinemanns – knows everyone – But could I ever know her?' There was a break in the relationship shortly after this of about a year, but soon Virginia was invited to Knole (Vita's family home, which, because she was female, she could not inherit) and to Long Barn where Vita lived with her husband Harold Nicolson and their two sons. By September 1924 Virginia was describing her in her diary as:

> a perfect lady, with all the dash & courage of the aristocracy, & less of its childishness than I expected. [...] She has shed the old verbiage, & comes to terms with some sort of glimmer of art; so I think; & indeed, I rather marvel at her skill, & sensibility; for is she not mother, wife, great lady, hostess, as well as scribbling?

Vita generously allowed the Woolfs to publish her novel *Seducers in Ecuador*, which came out in November 1924; the novel proved to be a bestseller, making the Hogarth Press a significant amount of money. This signalled a long-standing alliance with the press, and despite bigger advances from larger publishing houses Vita published thirteen of her many subsequent works with the Woolfs.

Their first sexual encounter was in December 1925, before Vita's departure to Persia. In her diary following the event, Virginia described her lover sensuously drawing out the differences between them:

> These Sapphists *love* women; friendship is never untinged with amorosity. [...] I like her & being with her, & the

splendour – she shines in the grocers shop in Sevenoaks with a candle lit radiance, stalking on legs like beech trees, pink glowing, grape clustered, pearl hung. That is the secret of her glamour, I suppose. [...] There is her maturity & full breastedness: her being so much in full sail on the high tides, where I am coasting down backwaters; her capacity I mean to take the floor in any company, to represent her country, to visit Chatsworth, to control silver, servants, chow dogs; her motherhood (but she is a little cold & off-hand with her boys) her being in short (what I have never been) a real woman.

Virginia's experience of Vita was of a woman in control of her body and life; she was glamorous, physically strong, a mother and a successful writer. And yet, in terms of her mind, Virginia always found her lacking: 'in brain & insight she is not as highly organised as I am'. This is perhaps partly why, when Vita won the Hawthornden Prize on 16th June 1927 for her long poem *The Land*, Virginia described the ceremony as 'a horrid show up'. Vita also played the maternal role that Virginia required of her sister and Leonard; she was protective of Virginia on their trip to Burgundy together in 1928. The weeklong trip was successful, though Virginia was 'excited, but afraid – she may find me out' and wrote every day to Leonard. This loving relationship with Vita, which had been building over the course of the decade, inspired Virginia's last novel of the 1920s, *Orlando* (1928).

Shortly after their first meeting, Virginia wrote to Vita claiming: 'There is nothing I enjoy more than family histories, so I am falling upon Knole the first moment I get.' Vita's history of her family home, *Knole and the Sackvilles* (1922), fascinated Virginia and it formed one of the early inspirations for *Orlando*. Virginia took much of her detail from it for use in the novel and it is possible to draw close parallels between certain facts and even descriptive passages in the two books. However, there were many other reasons why Virginia came to write her most extravagant and individual novel. During their friendship/love affair, Virginia was jealous of Vita's other young women, in particular Mary Campbell, wife of the South African poet Roy Campbell. Sensing that Vita's affections were slowly drifting away, Virginia cast about for a hook to bring her back, if not in body, then in mind. The novel was a seductive vision of Vita that would link the two women together regardless of husbands and Vita's torrid affairs. The novel was also penned as a dig at the old forms of biography (particularly her father's factual style), while exploring her interest in Sapphism and female relationships, and her desire to record the personalities of friends; and as a comfort for Vita who had lost her beloved family home on 28th January 1928 when her father died.

The first stirrings of the novel can be traced to a detailed diary entry of 14th March 1927:

> It struck me, vaguely, that I might write a Defoe narrative for fun. Suddenly between twelve & one I conceived a whole fantasy to be called 'The Jessamy Brides' – why, I wonder? I have rayed round it several scenes. Two women, poor, solitary at the top of a house. One can see anything (for this is all fantasy) the Tower Bridge, clouds, aeroplanes. Also old men listening in the room over the way. Everything is to be tumbled in pall mall. It is to be written as I write letters at the top of my speed: on the ladies of Llangollen; on Mrs Fladgate; on people passing. No attempt is to be made to realise the character. Sapphism is to be suggested. Satire is to be the main note – atire & wildness. The Ladies are to have Constantinople in view. Dreams of golden domes. My own lyric vein is to be satirised. Everything mocked. And it is to end with three dots … so. For the truth is I feel the need of an escapade after these serious poetic experimental books whose form is always so closely considered. I want to kick up my heels & be off.

She elaborated in a later entry of October 1927: 'a biography beginning in the year 1500 & continuing to the present day, called Orlando: Vita; only with a change about from one sex to another. I think, for a treat, I shall let myself dash this in for a week'. And to Vita she described how: 'I couldn't screw a word from me; and at last dropped my head in my hands: dipped my pen in the ink, and wrote these words, as if automatically, on a clean sheet: Orlando: A Biography. No sooner had I done this than my body was flooded with rapture and my brain with ideas. I wrote rapidly till 12.' She initially imagined it to be 'a small book, & written by Christmas', as light relief after her more serious experimental novels, and asked Vita's permission to write it. Vita responded positively, though realising that it might contain a snub or two as punishment for 'gallivanting down the lanes with Campbell':

> My God, Virginia, if ever I was thrilled and terrified it is at the prospect of being projected into the shape of Orlando. What fun for you; what fun for me. You see, any vengeance that you ever want to take will lie ready to your hand. Yes, do go ahead, toss up your pancake, brown it nicely on both sides, pour brandy over it, and serve it hot. You have my full permission. Only I think that having drawn and quartered me, unwound and retwisted me, or whatever it is that you intend to do, you ought to dedicate it to your victim.[27]

Orlando consisted of in-jokes and personal jibes, which were primarily meant to amuse and tease the knowing audience, but were also designed to disguise a layer of acid criticism. Vita was expected to be amused by her faults and Virginia even found the good grace to 'satirise' her 'own lyric vein'. Though fearfully close to spite at times, Virginia was able to defuse her criticism with either humour or flattery to the extent that Vita found herself exposed to 'a new form of narcissism – I confess,' she wrote, 'I am in love with Orlando.'[28] Vita was the eponymous hero/ine; Vita's real-life ex-lover, Violet Trefusis, was translated into a Russian princess; Lord Lascelles (who had asked Vita to marry him) became the Archduke/duchess Harry/Harriet Griselda of Finster-Aarhorn and Scandop-Boom; while places and events suffered similar mutations (even the private pet names used between Vita and Harold Nicolson appeared in the text). The conversion of real individuals into outrageous fictional characters was the central source of amusement to those in the know. Some reviewers of *Orlando* were immediately aware that Woolf's mock-biography required a familiarity with the real figures behind the fantasised characters in order to be fully appreciated. Conrad Aiken in his review for the Chicago *Dial* in February 1929 commented: 'Some of the references, it is true, are too esoteric – for one not in the enchanted circle – to be universally valid; and this may or may not be thought a mistake. One's private jokes and innuendoes are pretty apt to become meaningless, with the passage of time and the disappearance of the *milieu* which gave them point.'[29] One perceptive critic, writing for the *Daily Chronicle* in November 1928, realised that Woolf had managed to take a private joke and make it accessible, though not fully transparent to the general reader: 'The book in Bloomsbury is a joke, in Mayfair a necessity, and in America a classic.'[30]

It was also a joke at her father's expense, for one of Virginia's central aims in writing *Orlando* was to 'revolutionise biography in a night', though she was aware that the fictional form allowed her 'to get at the truth about a life as it is not possible to do if one writes a biography dealing with facts'.[31] With its preface, pictures, photographs and index, the structure of *Orlando* ostensibly belonged to biography, though the style of writing and the characters were fictional and the narrator-biographer continually stepped in to highlight the inadequacy of the form for the delineation of a human life, much of which is lived in the mind. The narrator points out:

Life, it has been agreed by everyone whose opinion is worth consulting, is the only fit subject for novelist or biographer; life, the same authorities have decided, has nothing whatever to do with sitting still in a chair and thinking. Thought and life are as the poles asunder. Therefore – since sitting in a chair and thinking is precisely what Orlando is doing now – there is nothing for it but to recite the calendar, tell one's beads, blow one's nose, stir the fire, look out of the window, until she has done.

In Virginia's opinion, biography had been reduced to prosaic hagiographies which, due to all the constraints of family censorship, often failed to represent the true life and personality of the individual in question. In her essay 'The New Biography' (1927), Virginia described the problem:

if we think of truth as something of granite-like solidity and of personality as something of rainbow-like intangibility and reflect that the aim of biography is to weld these two into one seamless whole, we shall admit that the problem is a stiff one and that we need not wonder if biographers, for the most part failed to solve it.

In order to remedy this issue, *Orlando* was designed to fuse fact with fiction, it was the life of Vita and the history of the Sackvilles, but it was also fictional and fantastical; a mock biography, mocking biography.

The novel was completed on 17th March 1928 and she wrote to Vita: 'ORLANDO IS FINISHED!!! Did you feel a sort of tug, as if your neck was being broken on Saturday last at 5 minutes to one? That was when he died – or rather stopped talking, with three little dots …' Although revisions followed, the book was written and published in only a year. Speed was the key to *Orlando*'s vitality – it was designed as 'a very quick brilliant book' written at a 'dash'. Depths were eschewed in favour of 'writing exteriorly', thus giving Virginia respite from the intensive psychological studies, *Mrs Dalloway* (1925) and *To the Lighthouse* (1927). *Orlando* was a writer's holiday: 'I have written this book quicker than any: & it is all a joke; & yet gay & quick reading I think; a writers holiday.' Though meant as a joke, Leonard read it and took it very seriously. She recorded his thoughts: '[Leonard] thinks it in some ways better than The Lighthouse; about more interesting things, & with more attachment to life, & larger [...] He says it is very original.' Though reviewed favourably, initial sales were slow because it was being shelved as biography, rather than fiction. 'A high price to pay for the fun of calling it a biography,' she noted in her diary. Virginia was also aware that the novel was being published at a time when Radclyffe Hall's *The Well of Loneliness*, an openly lesbian novel, was being prosecuted for obscenity in the British courts. Indeed, Virginia signed the letter by E.M. Forster to the *Nation* protesting against the potential ban and which argued that the book (though in Virginia's opinion a poor work of art), should be published partly on the basis of freedom of speech and partly because there were many more 'unpleasant' topics that novels could cover than sapphism. Virginia was to be called as an expert witness in the trial, but was relieved that her opinion was not in the end called upon. Nevertheless, the book was censored by the homophobic Sir Chartres Biron on 16th November 1928. Luckily for Virginia (and The Hogarth Press), the lesbian elements of *Orlando*, hidden behind the novel's playfulness and fantasy, were overlooked and the novel eventually outsold all of her previous works.

The last book of the 1920s was not a novel, but a long feminist tract about women and fiction, which was published as *A Room of One's Own* on 24th October 1929. Virginia had often noted and felt angered by the disparity between the treatment of women and men in the literary world, indeed the topic is hinted at both in *To the Lighthouse* and *Orlando*. In September 1920, she had railed against Bennett's collection of essays, *Our*

Women, which had argued that women are the intellectual inferiors of men, and she was angered by the support given to his argument by her friend Desmond MacCarthy as a columnist writing under the pseudonym Affable Hawk in the *New Statesman*. She defended the intellectual and creative potential of women in two letters printed in October 1920, which appeared in the *New Statesman* under the title of 'The Intellectual Status of Women'. Throughout the 1920s she returned to the idea, though she did not allow her anger to surface, fearing that it would undermine her efforts to be taken seriously as an author. This consciousness was outlined in *A Room of One's Own*:

> it is fatal for a woman to lay the least stress on any grievance; to plead even with justice any cause; in any way to speak consciously as a woman. And fatal is no figure of speech; for anything written with that conscious bias is doomed to death. It ceases to be fertilised. Brilliant and effective, powerful and masterly, as it may appear for a day or two, it must wither at nightfall; it cannot grow in the minds of others.

In February 1928 Virginia recorded: 'My mind is woolgathering away about Women & Fiction, which I am to read at Newnham'. Indeed, *A Room of One's Own* began as a lecture which she gave to Newnham College, Cambridge Arts Society on 20th October 1928 and Girton College, Cambridge ODTAA Society ('One Damn Thing After Another') on 26th October 1928. On her return from Girton she recorded: 'Starved but valiant young women – that's my impression. Intelligent eager, poor; & destined to become schoolmistresses in shoals. I blandly told them to drink wine & have a room of their own. Why should all the splendour, all the luxury of life be lavished on the Julians [...] And nobody respected me.' Her argument in the finished work revolved around four central points. Firstly, that women should be allowed to earn their own money and to have a well-kept space in which to do this in order to write fiction (unlike Jane Austen, who wrote in the communal sitting room); secondly, that women must create their own style of writing; thirdly, that they should write without anger (which, for Virginia, marred Brontë's *Jane Eyre*); and fourthly, she put forward the idea that great writers are androgynous, that they write as men and women, or forget their sex altogether. Ideally, she argued, gender should exist within every individual as a combination of masculine and feminine characteristics which was, she suggested, 'the normal and comfortable state of being'.

In June 1929 she was referring to it as 'that much corrected book' and worried prior to its publication that 'much is watery & flimsy & pitched in too high a voice'. She was concerned that there might be 'a shrill feminine tone' which would mean being 'attacked for a feminist' and would lead to the piece 'not be[ing] taken seriously'. In his review of the book for the *Evening Standard*, 28th November 1929, Arnold Bennett was characteristically disparaging of the book's argument and structure: 'whereas a woman cannot walk through a meadow in June without wandering all over the place to pick attractive blossoms, a man can. Virginia Woolf cannot resist the floral enticement.'[32] Today, however, *A Room of One's Own* is regarded as one of the seminal tracts of the feminist movement, though its author was fearful of the term. It also heralded the beginning of a new and stressful friendship with the composer and feminist activist Ethel Smyth, to whom she wrote:

I didnt write 'A room' without considerable feeling even you will admit; I'm not cool on the subject. And I forced myself to keep my own figure fictitious; legendary. If I had said, Look here am I uneducated, because my brothers used all the family funds which is the fact – Well theyd have said; she has an axe to grind; and no one would have taken me seriously, though I agree I should have had many more of the wrong kind of reader; who will read you and go away and rejoice in the personalities, not because they are lively and easy reading; but because they prove once more how vain, how personal, so they will say, rubbing their hands with glee, women always are; I can hear them as I write.

The 1930s

Well we are very happy. Life buds & sprouts all round us: by which I mean, everybody accepts if we ask them. Joyce Wethered would 'adore' to come; & on Tuesday Stephen Spender, Miss Lynd dine, & Plomer & K. Raine come in – all young, all new. And Vita lunches. And tomorrow I go to tea with the Richmonds. I think we live in a rich porous earth. I think we live very fully, freely, & adventurously.

– *The Diary of Virginia Woolf*

Virginia's fame as a novelist in the 1930s meant visitors; some were welcome, others were less so, such as a stranger with a note-book wanting an interview from whom she had to hide at Monk's House in March 1937. She was receiving written attention from a number of quarters: Winifred Holtby (1932), Floris Delattre (1932) and Ruth Grüber (1935) wrote books on her and doctoral students like Ingeborg Badenhausen (1932) began to research her work. When Grüber sent her study, Virginia described the impression: 'some good German woman sends me a pamphlet on me, into which I couldnt resist looking, though nothing so upsets & demoralises as this looking at ones face in the glass.' There were the usual mixture of critics and criticism which helped to raise her profile, though not always in the most positive ways. She came under attack from Wyndham Lewis in his novel *Apes of God* (1930) in which he satirized the Bloomsbury art scene, and in his book of essays entitled *Men Without Art* (1934) in which he claimed that Virginia's work was 'extremely insignificant' and that she wrote 'pretty salon pieces'. After further attacks by Lewis, Frank Swinnerton and St John Ervine, Virginia felt moved to write a defensive letter in March 1935, though it was never sent. She was offered honorary degrees from Manchester, which she turned down in spring 1933, and from Liverpool University, which she refused in spring 1939. She gave broadcast talks on writing, one with Leonard in 1927 entitled 'Are Too Many Books Written and Published', and two on her own ('Beau Brummell' in November 1929 and 'Words Fail Me' in April 1937). In 1930 she was Clio in Boris Anrep's mosaicked floor for the National Gallery; in July 1931 she sat for a sculpture by Stephen Tomlin and a painting by Vanessa, and was photographed by Man Ray in November 1934 and Gisèle Freund in June 1939, none of which she enjoyed, having taken little pleasure from her appearance for most of her life. She was annoyed that images of her had been used in Cecil Beaton's *The Book of Beauty* (1930) without her permission; and that an informal snapshot was to be published as the frontispiece to Holtby's book, not the more formal and flattering Lenare photograph. 'Privacy invaded; ugliness revealed' she growled, but she had already noted much earlier in 1928 that her celebrity was 'becoming vulgar & a nuisance'. However, scrutiny was the price of increasing fame and fortune.

She was finally earning enough money to allow herself little extravagancies. There were improvements to be made at Monk's House; a new car to be bought (the Lanchester); and she no longer needed to fret over the price of a £3 dress, claiming proudly: 'No more poverty I said; & poverty has ceased.' She encouraged herself 'to spend freely, without fuss or anxiety; & to trust to one's power of making more', though her loan of £150 to Roger Fry's widow, Helen Anrep, caused her a great deal of disquiet and she reduced Angelica's allowance when war broke out. In 1930 she was pleased to find her income equivalent to the salary of a civil servant. Though she spoke of poverty and retrenchment, the Woolfs were never poor. Virginia had been left money by her Aunt Caroline Stephen and her father, and she received a share of Stella's marriage settlement after her death which Stella's husband, Jack Hills, kindly restored to them until he remarried in 1931. Nevertheless, Virginia had inherited her father's terror of destitution and was married to a man who celebrated economy.

In the early 1930s, Virginia was working hard on two volumes: her seminal Modernist masterpiece *The Waves* (1931) and the second volume of *The Common Reader* (1932). The beginnings of *The Waves* can be traced as far back as September 1926 when she records in her diary seeing in her mind's eye 'a fin passing far out', which, in her later marginal note, she states is 'Perhaps The Waves or moths (Oct. 1929)'. As the idea progressed she envisaged 'a solitary woman musing[?] a book of ideas about life [...] It is to be an endeavour at something mystic, spiritual'. She was to return to this sense of mysticism existing within ordinary life throughout the formulation of the novel. On Monday 21st February 1927, Virginia recorded the germ of an idea:

Why not invent a new kind of play – as for instance
Woman thinks:...
He does.
Organ Plays.
She writes.
They say:
She sings:
Night speaks:
They miss
I think it must be something in this line – though I cant now see what. Away from facts: free; yet concentrated; prose yet poetry; a novel & a play.

This vague imagining links the novel with her 1927 essay, 'Poetry, Fiction and the Future', in which she describes her ideas for the novel of the future – a new form that will fuse poetry, prose and drama. *The Waves*, as a more coherent concept, was developed by a letter from Vanessa dated 3rd May 1927, in which she wrote to tell her sister about the huge moths at Cassis 'flying madly in circles round me and the lamp' and the death of one in particular that she had tried to catch. It was from this letter that she took the working title for her book, 'The Moths', and from which she derived its structure – six characters, like moths fluttering around life's flame. By November 1928 she had resolved: 'I am going to hold myself from writing till I have it impending in me: grown heavy in my mind like a ripe pear; pendant, gravid, asking to be cut or it will fall. The Moths still haunts me, coming, as they always do, unbidden, between tea & dinner'. She also began to see the book more clearly as partly poem, as well as prose fiction and drama: 'what I want now to do is to saturate every atom. [...] Why admit any thing to literature that is not poetry – by which I mean saturated?' However, in May 1929 she was feeling 'no great impulse; no fever; only a great pressure of difficulty' – the book was becoming increasingly hard to manage. 'I am not reeling it off; but sticking it down,' she moaned. 'Also, never, never, in my life, did I attack such a vague yet elaborate design; whenever I make a mark I have to think of its relation to a dozen others.'

Her concerns mounted: she was not sure about the style in December 1929; she was 'straining'; she wrote 'variations of every sentence; compromises; bad shots; possibilities; till [her] writing book' became 'a lunatic's dream'; and it still seemed, in February 1930, like a 'litter of fragments'. 'If ever a book drained me, this one does,' she lamented in March 1930. Nevertheless, there was 'splendour' and 'greatness' in its form, a sense of completeness, she began to 're-write it, & conceive it again with ardour', 'reading much of it aloud, like poetry'. Throughout the process she took inspiration not only from her reading (Byron, Dante, Hazlitt, Shelley, Shakespeare), but also from Beethoven, which may explain her claim that she was 'writing The Waves to a rhythm not to a plot'. Indeed, she wrote that she wanted to 'make prose move [...] as prose has never moved before: from the chuckle & the babble to the rhapsody.'

The book, slowly and painstakingly, became a series of 'dramatic soliloquies' voiced by six friends, between which Virginia wrote 'interludes' that described the passage of the sun on a single day – a symbol of the characters' life cycle. There is no conventional plot, no narrative voice, just the verbalized impressions of the six characters as they express their thoughts, feelings and experiences. It had taken five years to get from initial impression to novel, though the actual writing of it took a little over two years. She noted her relief on finishing in her diary and sent letters to Edward Sackville-West and John Lehmann (who managed the Hogarth Press from 1931–2 and bought out Virginia's share in 1938) claiming that she wrote much of the novel 'in a kind of trance'. In her diary she described how she had 'reeled across the last ten pages with some moments of such intensity & intoxication that I seemed only to stumble after my own voice, or almost, after some sort of speaker (as when I was mad). I was almost afraid, remembering the voices that used to fly ahead.' Leonard read the final version in July 1931; he called it 'a masterpiece' though he also thought 'the first 100 pages extremely difficult' and was 'doubtful how far any common reader will follow'. 'But Lord!' she exclaimed, 'what a relief!'

When *The Waves* was published on 8th October 1931 there was the usual vacillation between thinking the novel very poor when she received negative comments from Hugh Walpole, which left her 'trembling under the sense of complete failure', and very good, such as when Goldsworthy Lowes Dickinson, John Lehmann and E.M. Forster wrote to praise it. Dickinson enthused:

Your book is a poem, and as I think a great poem. Nothing that I know of has ever been written like it. [...] The beauty of it is almost incredible. Such prose has never been written and it also belongs to here and now though it is dealing also with a theme that is perpetual and universal.[33]

She noted with amazement that, contrary to her expectations, the book was selling: 'Really, this unintelligible book is being better "received" than any of them. A note in The Times proper – the first time this has been allowed me. And it sells – how unexpected, how odd that people can read that difficult grinding stuff!'

The Waves secured her place in the literary firmament and elicited a request from Trinity College, Cambridge in February 1932 to deliver the Clark Lectures, an offer that she turned down because it would mean giving up her own writing for too long and would also mean undermining her criticism of the university system; though she admitted that her father, who had given the lectures in 1888, would have been very proud:

This, I suppose, is the first time a woman has been asked; & so it is a great honour – think of me, the uneducated child reading books in my room at 22 H.P.G. – now advanced to this glory. But I shall refuse: because how could I write 6 lectures, to be delivered in full term, without giving up a year to criticism; without becoming a functionary; without sealing my lips when it comes to tilting at Universities; without putting off my Knock at the Door; without perhaps shelving another novel. [...] And I am pleased; & still more pleased that I wont do it; & like to think that father would have blushed with pleasure could I have told him 30 years ago, that his daughter – my poor little Ginny – was to be asked to succeed him: the sort of compliment he would have liked.

These lectures were, to Virginia at least, a symbol of the predominantly male, elitist academic establishment from which she, as a woman, had been excluded. The lectures would, she states, have forced her to become a 'functionary' of criticism and would have meant 'sealing my lips when it comes to tilting at universities' – a hypocrisy Virginia was unwilling to practise. Her anger against the university system found vent in her letters, essays, lectures (including 'Professions for Women' which was given to the National Society for Women's Service on 21st January 1931) and her later feminist tract *Three Guineas* (1938). The Clark Lectures also represented the antithesis of her projects in *The Common Reader*, which sought to appeal to individuals who had, like herself, been excluded from the hallowed corridors of Oxbridge.

'Why did I ever say I would produce another volume of Common Reader?' she asked her diary in February 1932. 'It will take me week after week, month after month. However a year spent – save for diversions in Greece & Russia – in reading through English literature will no doubt do good to my fictitious brain. Rest it anyhow. One day, all of a rush, fiction will burst in.' *The Common Reader: Second Series* was partly written as a means to encourage Virginia's creative outputs as she claimed, but also as a response to the elitist literary criticism of her peers and predecessors. It was (along with her other work) meant to 'reach a far wider circle,' she wrote to Benedict Nicolson, 'than a little private circle of exquisite and cultivated people.' The two volumes of essays were also a partial resolution (along with *To the Lighthouse*) of her troubled relationship with her father, whose style of literary criticism she both respected and disliked. She was uncomfortable with the formal style in which the articles were written, and wished, even as she was writing the volume of criticism in November 1931, that she could 'devise a new critical method; something far less stiff & formal than these Times articles. But I must keep to the old style in this volume. And how, I wonder, could I do it? There must be some simpler, subtler, closer means of writing about books, as about people, could I hit upon it.' After its publication on 13th October 1932, she confided to William Rothenstein: 'I always feel apologetic about publishing my own criticism, because I dont know that there is much excuse for adding to books about other books'. (It was a sentiment that caused a storm when she questioned the need for reviewers in her much later pamphlet *Reviewing* in 1939.) She turned to another project as light relief from the difficulty of *The Waves* and the dryness of *The Common Reader*. This was *Flush* (1933), a comic biography of the poet Elizabeth Barrett Browning's pet spaniel. In August 1931 she recorded 'writing Flush of a morning, half seriously to ease my brain, knotted by all that last screw of The Waves'. But even this 'freak of writing' was laboured over and she worried that it would be dismissed as 'ladylike'. It was published on 5th October 1933, praised by the *TLS* and *New Statesman & Nation*, but criticized by Rebecca West in *The Daily Telegraph* and by reviewers in *The Morning Post* and *Granta*.

These books were written against the background of a political scene that was becoming increasingly volatile. The 1930s were overshadowed by the rise of Hitler in Germany, Mussolini in Italy and the Spanish Civil War. Europe was preparing for war again, though every effort was made by the British Prime Minister, Neville Chamberlain, to avoid it. The Night of the Long Knives in June 1934, on which Hitler had his political opponents murdered, was described in her diary with anger and a sense of trepidation for what was to come: 'these brutal bullies go about in hoods & masks, like little boys dressed up, acting this idiotic, meaningless, brutal, bloody, pandemonium. [...] And here we sit, Osbert [Sitwell] I &c, remarking this is inconceivable. [...] And for the first time I read articles with rage, to find him [Hitler] called a real leader.' Politics were discussed with the Wigrams; with Kingsley Martin; with Keynes, who had worked for the Treasury during the First World War; with Lord Cecil, who argued that the League of Nations had failed; with the exiled German composer Bruno Walter; it hung like a black cloud over the conversation at parties.

The events unfolding in Europe led her towards writing an anti-fascist pamphlet, which was first discussed with Leonard in

February 1935 and fed into *Three Guineas*. It also led her towards becoming a committee member of the anti-fascist exhibition and she was initially involved in the International Association of Writers for the Defence of Culture. The political climate led Leonard into writing a number of books on the situation unfolding in Europe and pushed them both to attend a conference on peace held in October 1935; meetings of the group 'For Intellectual Liberty' in February 1936, as well as the usual Labour party conferences and meetings; and to sign letters and telegrams protesting about what the fascists were doing in Europe. In June 1931 Leonard finished the first volume of his book, *After the Deluge*, that he had been working on for most of the 1920s, after which he was also asked to give six broadcast talks on politics. Four years later, in May 1935, he published *Quack! Quack!*, which offered a direct attack on fascism, and in November he was woken 'by a man shouting abuse of Woolf & Quack in German under his window'. They took a road tour of Europe in May 1935 (they had also visited Fascist Italy in 1933), during which they drove through Nazi Germany, where they saw anti-Jewish banners and got caught up in a reception for Goering. She recorded the event in her diary:

> They cheered Mitzi [the Woolfs' pet marmoset which they bought in July 1934]. I raised my hand. People gathering in the sunshine – rather forced like school sports. Banners stretched across the street 'The Jew is our Enemy' 'There is no place for Jews in –'. So we whizzed along until we got out of range of the docile hysterical crowd. Our obsequiousness gradually turning to anger. Nerves rather frayed. A sense of stupid mass feeling masked by good temper.

The growing tensions in Europe contributed to Virginia's precarious mental state, though this was by no means the only cause of her health problems in the 1930s. There were fainting fits at Monk's House (1930 and 1932) and The Ivy (1932), the usual headaches and a sense of 'inane pointlessness [...] of things generally wrong in the universe'. Along with the situation in Europe, these issues were caused by the deaths of close friends, the awareness of her own ageing and 'time of life' and concomitant fear of obsoleteness, which left her feeling 'as if I were drumming slightly in the veins: very cold: impotent: & terrified. As if I were exposed on a high ledge in full light'. The most taxing events for Virginia mentally were the completion of her difficult novels *The Waves* and particularly *The Years*; though in spite of these mental glitches she still managed to shout 'Death I defy you' to her diary.

Though she remained defiant in her rejection of her own illness, the decade was marred by a number of significant deaths, which contributed to her growing sense of melancholy. Among the literati were D.H. Lawrence who died in March 1930 (they had never met, but she had respected his work); Arnold Bennett, her old sparring partner who died in 1931 and whose funeral she attended in March; John Galsworthy (February 1933); Stella Benson (December 1933); and W.B. Yeats (January 1939). Among the family there were George Duckworth (April 1934) whom she momentarily remembered more kindly commenting sadly 'how childhood goes with him'; Gerald Duckworth (September 1937) whom she had described at their last meeting as 'an alligator in a tank, an obese & obsolete alligator'; Jack Hills (December 1938); and Leonard's mother (July 1939) who had been a ridiculous and oppressive presence demanding sympathy and visits, which led Virginia to confide to her diary that 'everyone would be relieved if she could make an end of it' – she obliged a few days later. Close friends were also departing: Charlie Sanger (February 1930); Lytton Strachey (January 1932); Goldsworthy Lowes Dickinson (August 1932); Roger Fry (September 1934); Francis Birrell (January 1935); Janet Case (July 1937); Lady Ottoline Morrell (April 1938); and Ka Arnold-Forster (May 1938). Goldie's death led Virginia to reflect on her own mortality: 'I get the strangest feeling now of our all being in the midst of some vast operation: of the splendour of this undertaking – life: of being capable of dying: an immensity surrounds us.' She vowed 'not to let friends lapse [...] these are the little efforts I make against death'. Lytton Strachey and Roger Fry's deaths were particularly difficult to bear. Lytton's book *Portraits in Miniature and Other Essays* had appeared in May 1931, and Virginia's praise of it was warm: 'Lytton's book: very good. Thats his line. The compressed yet glowing account which requires logic, reason, learning, taste, wit order & infinite skill – this suits him far better, I think than the larger scale, needing boldness, originality, sweep.' Sadly, it shortly after transpired that Lytton was dying of stomach cancer and the Woolfs spent a dreary Christmas worried about their old friend. Lytton eventually died on 21st January 1932 and, as usual, Virginia re-envisaged him in her diary:

I see him coming along the street, muffled up with his beard resting on his tie: how we should stop: his eyes glow. Now I am too numb with all the emotion yesterday to do more than think thoughts like this. Well, as I know, the pain will soon begin. One toys about with this & that. How queer it was last night at the party, the tightness round everyone's lips – ours I mean. Duncan Nessa & I sobbing together in the studio – the man looking out of the mews window – a sense of something spent, gone.

Dora Carrington, who had first moved in with Lytton in 1917, and had loved him despite his homosexuality, was suicidal after his death. Virginia and Leonard went to Ham Spray to talk to her in March 1932, but she shot herself the day after they visited. In April 1932, as a moment of respite from Lytton's and Carrington's deaths, the Woolfs travelled to Greece with Roger and Margery Fry. It was a very different journey to the one Virginia had been on with her siblings and Violet Dickinson in 1906 and less eventful than the later one through Nazi Germany. She enjoyed Roger's company immensely, stating in a letter to

Ethel Smyth that he was 'far and away the best admirer of life and art I've ever travelled with'. Two years later, Roger died from a fall at his home leaving Virginia with the greatest sense of emptiness: 'Yes, his death is worse than Lytton's. Why I wonder? Such a blank wall. Such a silence. Such a poverty. How he reverberated! And I feel it through Nessa.' She worried about death and the slow loss of friends and family and as an antidote to this she took on Roger's biography which she worked on, initially excitedly but often reluctantly, for most of the 1930s; it was also suggested that she should write Lytton's life, but this project never took off.

Though darkened by the deaths of so many friends, the 1930s did see several new friendships forming: with the younger novelist Elizabeth Bowen whom Virginia initially found too retiring, but with whom she eventually became intimate (they visited her at her family estate in Ireland in 1934); with the Argentinian editor, feminist and writer Victoria Ocampo ('with eyes like the roe of codfish phosphorescent'); and, more significantly, with the composer and feminist Ethel Smyth. Virginia met Ethel on 20th February 1930 after she had read A Room of One's Own. Virginia recorded their first meeting with some amusement in her diary: 'I was lying here at four yesterday when I heard the bell ring then a brisk tramp up the stairs; & then behold a bluff, military old woman (older than I expected) bounced into the room, a little glazed flyaway & abrupt; in a three cornered hat & tailor made suit.' Virginia felt, as she wrote to her nephew Quentin Bell, as though she had been 'caught by a giant crab'. She was forced to sit through Ethel's operas, The Prison (February 1931) and The Wreckers (October 1931, though she had seen it in 1909), and her Mass in D performed in March 1934 to honour Ethel's seventy-five years. The composer's personality began to rankle with Virginia following a series of arguments: 'I do not like Ethel when she is doing the powerful stunt – or whatever stunt it is: proclaiming that all is over; denouncing me; protesting her love; whipping up a scene; being August;

despairing; melodramatic, & wobbly & weak all at the same time. No I do not like it: & also I am bored.' They argued over 'Bloomsbury' when Ethel sneered at it; Virginia ordered her only half-jokingly to 'never come and see me, who live in Bloomsbury, again'. Leonard found her company unbearable. Ethel, though frustratingly demanding, overly talkative and with a somewhat mistaken belief in her own genius, was also a confidante. It was to Ethel that Virginia explained her experiences with the Duckworth brothers at 22 Hyde Park Gate; her madness; and her feminist beliefs. She stated succinctly in one letter to Ethel: 'women alone stir my imagination'; and she used her as inspiration for the suffragette Rose Pargiter in *The Years* and for the director Miss La Trobe in *Between the Acts*.

Ethel arrived at the beginning of the cooling of Vita and Virginia's friendship. Virginia began to dislike the way that Vita wrote for money: 'pray heaven' she begged in January 1932, 'I may never fall into the money-trap!'; she saw cracks in Vita's physical appearance; she was hurt that Vita had gone on holiday with Hilda Matheson without informing her; she was jealous of her relationship with Gwen St Aubyn; and lost faith in her ability to choose worthwhile friends. By March 1935 she was writing: the 'friendship with Vita is over. Not with a quarrel, not with a bang, but as ripe fruit falls. [...] And there is no bitterness, & no disillusion, only a certain emptiness.' This is not a strictly accurate portrayal of their relationship in the 1930s; certainly they ceased to be sexually involved and saw less of one another, but affectionate letters ('one of the very few constant presences is your's' she wrote to Vita in August 1939) and the fact that Vita was deemed to be the most important person to inform of Virginia's death after close family, suggest otherwise. Vita kept a photograph of Virginia on her writing desk for the rest of her life.

Throughout most of these deaths and turbulent friendships, Virginia was writing 'The Pargiters', which was eventually split into two works and published as *The Years* (1937) and *Three Guineas* (1938). In January 1931, while in the midst of *The Waves*,

Virginia had formulated a new novel: 'I'm very much excited,' she claimed. The novel was called a number of different names during its development: 'Here and Now', 'Music', 'Dawn', 'Sons and Daughters', 'Daughters and Sons', 'Ordinary People', 'The Caravan', 'Other People's Houses' – *The Years* was finally decided on in 1935. She started writing the 'essay-novel', as it was initially envisaged, in October 1932: 'its to take in everything, sex, education, life &c; & come, with the most powerful & agile leaps, like a chamois across precipices from 1880 to here & now – Thats the notion anyhow, & I have been in such a haze & dream & intoxication, declaiming phrases, seeing scenes'. By December 1932 she had written 60,320 words, according to her diary, and mistakenly claimed that it was the 'quickest' of her books, 'easy' in comparison with *The Waves*. She found herself speaking the novel, rehearsing it like a play, to which she compared it in June 1933. In April 1933 she had a clear idea of what she wanted to achieve:

I think this will be a terrific affair. I must be bold & adventurous. I want to give the whole of the present society – nothing less: facts, as well as the vision. And to combine them both. I mean, The Waves going on simultaneously with Night & Day. Is this possible? At present I have assembled 50,000 words of 'real' life: now in the next 50 I must somehow comment; Lord knows how – while keeping the march of events. The figure of Elvira is the difficulty. She may become too dominant. She is to be seen only in relation to other things. This should give I think a great edge to both of the realities – this contrast. At present, I think the run of events is too fluid & too free. It reads thin; but lively. How am I to get the depth without becoming static? But I like these problems, & anyhow theres a wind & a vigour in this naturalness. It should aim at immense breadth & immense intensity. It should include satire, comedy, poetry, narrative, & what form is to hold them all together? Should I bring in a play, letters, poems? I think I begin to grasp the whole. And its to end with the press of daily normal life continuing. And there are to be millions of ideas but no preaching – history, politics, feminism, art, literature – in short a summing up of all I know, feel, laugh at, despise, like, admire hate & so on.

The Years was initially meant to alternate fictional episodes with essays on class, politics and feminism, but the fusion of these two antithetical styles failed. She split the essay-novel in two. The Years became a fictional family epic charting the life of the Pargiter family from 1880 to the present day, which looked obliquely at the socio-political issues that had been bothering her, and Three Guineas became a much revised synthesis of the essays. As she wrote she began to find the novel 'all too shrill & voluble'; she was afraid of it becoming didactic, a tone which she believed had nothing to do with art. It was also becoming an 'immense length', much of which needed to be rewritten. Though the last words were put down in October 1934, Virginia took two years to revise the manuscript.

As a break from writing, Virginia resurrected an earlier project; her only play, Freshwater. The first draft of the play, which was written in 1923, had offered a welcome distraction from Mrs Dalloway and the second would prove to offer the same break from The Years. In a diary entry of 1934 Virginia recorded: 'I'm in the thick again. But I will stop at the end of the funeral scene [in The Years], & calm my brain. That is I will write the play for Xmas: Freshwater a farce – for a joke.' The play was a skit on the Victorians and satirized their hero-worship of great men, in this instance, the painter G.F. Watts (played by Duncan) and the poet Alfred Lord Tennyson (played by Adrian), as well as her own eccentric great-aunt, Julia Margaret Cameron (played by Vanessa). In Freshwater, the young and beautiful actress Ellen Terry (played by Angelica) who is married to the ageing Watts, runs off with an attractive young naval lieutenant called John Craig (played by Julian). Following the production in Vanessa's London studio in January 1935, she stated to her cousin, the actress Virginia Isham, that the piece 'was to amuse my sisters children' and 'a mere Christmas scrap'. Though she designed it as a joke, like *Flush*, the play was rewritten in order to make it more substantial; it addressed a number of Virginia's favourite themes and the criticism of it after the performance was dissected in her diary as usual. Quentin Bell describes in his biography of Virginia how his father and Uncle Cory 'laughed so loud and so long that the dialogue was practically inaudible'.[34]

Despite this light aside, Virginia felt that *The Years* was a failure. She found the pressure of rewriting immense; she broke down, stating to her diary: 'never been so near the precipice to my own feeling since 1913' – the flimsiness of her diary for 1936 attested to her state of mind. In 1936, the novel was interrupted and influenced by the death of King George V, whose funeral she described to her nephew Julian as 'a curious survival of barbarism', and the Abdication Crisis. The event undermined the monarchy in Virginia's eyes, while George VI's coronation in 1937 led her to reflect on the emptiness of patriarchal pomp and ceremony. When Virginia finished the novel shortly after the crisis, she gave it to Leonard to read. He privately thought it the weakest of her books, though he told her that it was 'most remarkable'; that he liked it more than *The Waves*; that 'it must be published'. His lie was designed to avoid the serious mental collapse that he feared the novel was forcing her towards. 'Once out', she reassured herself, 'I will never look at it again. Its like a long childbirth.' She worried about the book's reception: 'I'm going to be beaten, I'm going to be laughed at,' she predicted, and yet they had sold over 5,000 copies prior to publication. On its appearance in March 1937, she was surprised and pleased to find the novel positively received by the *TLS*, *Time & Tide*, the *Evening Standard* and the *New Statesman & Nation*; though she was 'damnably depressed & smacked on the cheek' by reviews in *The Listener* and *The London Mercury*. It became a bestseller, topping the list for a number of months. The immense pressure of writing this lengthy novel caused her to claim in June 1937: 'I am doubtful if I shall ever write another novel.' Nevertheless, sales meant that the Hogarth Press was now worth £10,000 and she reflected with pride that 'all this sprung from that type on the drawing room table at Hogarth House 20 years ago.'

Though Virginia was now well-established, she was increasingly aware that the younger generation of poets (Stephen Spender, Christopher Isherwood, Cecil Day Lewis, W.H. Auden, Louis MacNeice) were also clamouring to be heard. She invited Spender to tea in October 1932: 'He is a rattle headed bolt eyed young man, raw boned, loose jointed who thinks himself the greatest poet of all time. I daresay he is – it's not a subject that interests me enormously at the moment.' Isherwood was 'rather a find'; Day Lewis 'sturdy' and 'truculent'; Auden, whom she met in 1937 at a meeting of the National Joint Committee for Spanish Relief, was a 'terrier man [...] interesting, I expect'. In response to their politicised poetry and drama she wrote *A Letter to a Young Poet* (1932) and 'The Leaning Tower' (1940), which criticized 'the 'loud-speaker strain' in their work. Her nephew, Julian Bell, was one of these politically minded young men with whom Virginia had a complex personal and literary relationship. Julian had the legacy of Bloomsbury to live up to, but was not (according to him) provided with the tools or abilities to have a respectable career. He failed to get a Cambridge fellowship in April 1933 with his dissertation on Alexander Pope (Keynes thought it 'uneducated') and, though he began another on philosophical questions, he did not succeed. Julian's collection of poems entitled *Winter Movement* (1930) was published by Chatto and Windus and, though it was generally well-received, Virginia was pleased that Vita agreed with her that the poems were poor: 'for all his admirable good sense & observation & love of country life, he is no poet. People who treat words as he does rather afflict me'. He also tried to get the Hogarth Press to print his poetry, but it was not good enough in the Woolfs' eyes to be published. Vanessa kindled and defended her son, much to Virginia's interest and annoyance, but his work was still refused. Eventually Julian accepted a professorship at Wuhan University in China and left to take it up in August 1935. 'I'm very sorry he's to go –' Virginia reflected, 'the delightful, honest bubbly yet after all so sympathetic & trusty young man.' While in China he entered into a close correspondence with the Woolfs and Vanessa. Vanessa wrote him 'love-letters', he sent her Chinese silks. He also sent Virginia 'A Letter to A' about Roger Fry, which he hoped to have published by the Hogarth Press, but when Virginia explained in June 1936 why they could not publish the essay, Julian was hurt and did not respond for a number of months. David 'Bunny' Garnett suspected Virginia of jealousy and Vanessa passed his opinion on to Julian in a letter:

> I do think there's something odd in the Woolves' attitude – which I discussed with Bunny [...] His theory is that V. lives so precariously (in nerves and brain) that she can't face any other writer of any real merit. The responsibility and strain of accepting them would somehow upset her own balance, he thinks. That is why she always gives absurd praise to obscure females.[35]

Julian was also worrying them all with his increasingly extreme political views and talk of going to fight in Spain against General Franco (a complete break from his old pacifist leanings). Vanessa wrote asking him to consider his decisions carefully: 'I should understand your wanting to go to Spain if you were here, only I do think nearly all war is madness. It's destruction and not creation and it's mad to destroy the best things and people';[36] 'you have a better intelligence than most people, and so it should be used, and not destroyed by a chance bullet.'[37] When he resigned from his position in Wuhan (partly because of an affair with a colleague's wife and partly because of his desire to participate in political events), Vanessa pleaded with him to return to England to discuss his decision to join the International Brigade before taking any further action. Virginia thought him 'dog obstinate' and wrote to Stephen Spender, who had already witnessed the conflict: 'I feel that its a mistake his going to Spain, but its no good saying so. I dont suppose he would see my arguments.' Julian refused to abandon his ambition of going to Spain, but he agreed to compromise by becoming an ambulance driver rather than a soldier. He left on 6th June 1937, but sadly, as Vanessa and Virginia had predicted, he died on 18th July 1937 from a shrapnel wound while driving an ambulance in the battle of Brunete – he was twenty-nine. Virginia had visions of her brother Thoby's death and described the loss of Julian in her diary as 'a complete break; almost a blank; like a blow on the head: a shrivelling up', and wrote how she felt 'floored by the complete muddle & waste'. She considered that 'the future without Julian is cut off. lopped: deformed'– an opinion shared by Vanessa. Vanessa was devastated; she would, she said, be 'cheerful, but I shall never be happy again'. Clive, Quentin and Angelica were also bereft (Angelica doubly confused as she was told the truth about her parentage that summer). In the sub-sequent months Virginia became a valuable support to Vanessa, who revealed her gratitude to Virginia via Vita Sackville-West, unable to express her feelings about Virginia's help directly: 'I heard about Julian lying in an unreal state and hearing her voice going on and on keeping life going as it seemed when otherwise it would have stopped, and late every day she came to see me here, the only point in the day one could want to come.'[38] In the major crises of Vanessa's life (her appendicitis (1906), miscarriage (1911), Duncan's pneumonia (1927), Roger's death (1934)) Virginia had always managed to be supportive and level-headed; the death of her nephew revealed this unexpected strength once again.

Julian's death was preceded by the publication of *The Years* and succeeded by the publication of *Three Guineas* and *Julian Bell:*

Essays, Poems and Letters edited by his brother Quentin in 1938. *Three Guineas* was, like *The Years*, given a number of different working titles: 'Professions for Women', 'The Open Door', 'Opening the Door', 'A Tap at the Door', 'Men are Like That', 'On Being Despised', 'The Next War', 'What Are We to Do?', 'Answers to Correspondents', 'Letter to an Englishman', 'Two Guineas'. The piece was written as a response to the rise of fascism, class differences and the place of women in this political climate, but it was also inspired by a number of other events and individuals, such as the General Strike of 1926; her old arguments with Julian Bell; and Virginia's feminist talk with Ethel Smyth to the London and National Society for Women's Service (which she joined in 1932) in January 1931: 'I have this moment, while having my bath, conceived an entire new book – a sequel to a Room of Ones Own – about the sexual life of women: to be called Professions for Women perhaps – Lord how exciting! This sprang out of my paper to be read on Wednesday to Pippa's society.' All through the 1930s she had been keeping a scrapbook of the inequalities between men and women, which she used as background research for both *The Years* and *Three Guineas*. She was so angered by E.M. Forster, who told her in April 1935 that women were not allowed on the library committee for the London Library, that her pen shook when writing out the encounter in her diary and she vowed to put the conversation in the pamphlet. She was scathing of the university system, and her refusal of honorary professorships and the Clark Lectures allowed her to attack the higher education system without hypocrisy in this tract. 'If we [women] are asked to lecture we can refuse to bolster up the vain and vicious system of lecturing by refusing to lecture', she vociferated, and 'medals, honours, degrees' must be 'refuse[d] [...] absolutely, since they are all tokens that culture has been prostituted and intellectual liberty sold into captivity'. The book also offered her the chance to outline an idea that had been surfacing and resurfacing since adolescence – the concept of the 'outsider'. The figure of the female outsider was meant to unify women into a rejection of dictatorial male government and its warmongering; it was a call to women for pacifism. The book had been simmering in the back of her mind for a number of years: 'It has pressed & spurted out of me, if thats any proof of virtue, like a physical volcano. And my brain feels cool & quiet after the expulsion. I've had it sizzling now since – well I was thinking of it at Delphi I remember.' The style and structure of the essay were, like *A Room of One's Own*, difficult to pin down, it was full of digressions and visions, questions and images. When she gave the script to Leonard he was unenthusiastic, warning her that she should expect negative responses from men (and from women, she added), but it was ultimately a pacifist position that he could not condone. She responded in her diary: '[I] have a quiet composed feeling; as if I had my say: take it or leave it' and considered it to have 'some importance [...] industry; fertility'.

The reception of *The Years* led Virginia to think that *Three Guineas*, which appeared on 2nd June 1938, would 'strike very sharp & clear on a hot iron', but initial reactions were slow and mixed:

> Mrs Lynd in Harper's Bazaar sneers, says I preach sitting still on a sofa; & Miss Osler or some such name writes to thank & praise – my grand work &c &c. These first rumours always give the shape of whats to come: I can foretell that those who dislike will sneer at me for a well to do aesthete; & those who approve will echo Rhondda's 'most exciting' profoundly moving.

It certainly provoked debate. In an amusing letter to her fifteen-year-old niece Philippa Woolf, Virginia jokingly dismissed the work as 'a pamphlet to make people angry and say irritating things', but critics took it more seriously. Q.D. Leavis wrote a very negative review accusing Virginia of aiming her theories only at women of her class; of making 'dangerous assumptions', 'preposterous claims'; and of having 'nasty attitudes'.[39] Virginia was also stung by the ambivalence of Vita who wrote to say that she felt the piece contained 'misleading arguments'. However, this criticism was leavened by more positive responses from Jane Walker, Nelly Cecil, Philippa Strachey and Emmeline Pethick Lawrence; all wrote in praise of what Virginia envisaged for the next generation of English women. In a symbolic gesture, she later sent the manuscript version to May Sarton to be sold for the relief of refugees and later still mooted the idea of writing another book on women and peace.

After the publication of *Three Guineas* the sense that war was about to break out overshadowed everything. They were waiting, preparing, poised: 'at any moment the guns may go off & explode us [...] Hitler has his hounds only very lightly held.' It became a 'grumble [...] behind reality'; 'a kind of perceptible but anonymous friction', she wrote in July 1939. Her thoughts were increasingly drawn towards death, though she was 'warmed' in April 1939 'by L. saying last night that he was fonder of me than I of him. A discussion as to which would mind the other's death most. He said he depended more upon our common life than I did [...] I was very happy to think I was so much needed.' They planned suicide in their garage in the event of a Nazi invasion and, as it turned out, both she and Leonard were on the Nazis' blacklist. War eventually came on 3rd September 1939.

The Final Years

On 6th September 1939 it seemed 'an empty meaningless world' where 'all creative power is cut off'. The war had only been declared three days previously, but the build up to it had taken almost a decade and had left Virginia in a state of nervous tension. She felt in Rodmell that they were living 'on a small sunny island – outside wastes of gloom and dark'. The full force of the war did not reach England until the summer of 1940, but they lived every day expecting invasion or air attack and Virginia immediately felt acute 'despair' at the situation – her hand began to tremble. The blackout made her feel that they were living like 'rats in caves' and that she was walking through 'tunnels of gloom'. They 'listened to the ravings, the strangled hysterical sobbing swearing ranting of Hitler'. As well as the sense of physical danger from German forces (she asked herself 'Am I a coward? Physically I expect I am'), she was also aware that with rationing and rising costs, including the price of paper, the Hogarth Press would suffer. They had already considered that war might mean the end of their publishing house as early as April 1939. She had written to Ling Su-Hua, a friend of Julian Bell's during his time in China, that 'It is very difficult to go on working under such uncertainty.' In the first month of the war she wrote to Ethel: 'ruin stares us in the face; and I begin to be stingy.' She warned Angelica that her allowance was to be cut back and wrote on both sides of her pages, but this retrenchment was alleviated when she received over £1,000 on the death of Jack Hills and by Vita's generous gifts of butter and wool. To make more money, she began 'slipping into the frying pan of journalism', but she was criticized for her article on reviewing ('all reviewers have their knives in me,' she wrote to Lady Simon Shena in November 1939). It became increasingly apparent at the end of 1939 that the only way she could contribute to the war effort was by writing; she told her niece Judith Stephen: 'I'm more and more convinced that it is our duty to catch Hitler in his home haunts and prod him if even with only the end of an old inky pen.' The following summer she was even more explicit: 'Thinking is my fighting.' Leonard took a similar tack by giving twelve Wednesday evening lectures to the Workers' Educational Association between 1st November 1939 and 10th April 1940 on 'Causes and Issues of the War'; he published *Barbarians at the Gate* in December 1939 and wrote a short book entitled *The War for Peace* published in September 1940, both for the Labour Book Club. Clearly, both Leonard and Virginia saw their pens and their position as leading avant-garde publishers as the best way to undermine fascism. Virginia's 'only relief' in the first months of war, she wrote to Ethel (who was in the process of falling in love with her eighty-one-year-old next-door neighbour), was that her nephew Quentin was 'employed safely driving a tractor – rejected by the army'.

As war broke out she was forcing her brain to work on the biography of her old friend, Roger Fry, but she noted that 'force is the dullest of experiences'. The project had begun shortly after his death in 1934 when it had seemed 'a splendid, difficult chance' to try her hand at serious biography; 'better than trying to find a subject' she had noted on 12th November 1934. She also felt an element of obligation and was annoyed that she had been asked to give the opening address at the memorial exhibition of his work on 12th July 1935. She had spent much of her time reading his papers and trying to find a suitable method. 'Why not begin at the end [...] & then work backwards: [...] give specimen days, all through his life,' she mooted, and considered asking different people to write each of the chapters. She was sent boxes 'full of tailor's bills love letters and old picture postcards'; she visited his houses and old haunts; she conducted interviews with family and friends. Virginia was well aware that Roger's family stood over his memory guarding it from unpleasant truths, such as his experiences of homosexuality in Cambridge; the love affair with Vanessa; and his annoyance at Clive Bell for pilfering his ideas on art. 'Roger had,' according to Marjorie Strachey, 'no life that [could] be written.' Virginia reflected, 'I daresay this is true.' 'How does one square the relatives? How does one euphemise 20 different mistresses?' she asked Ethel.

She began to write the biography in 1938, incorporating some of her nephew Julian's essay on Roger that she had refused to publish while Julian was alive. Though frequently referring to the biography as 'drudgery' and a 'grind', it did give her a break from thinking about the war and presented her with a new understanding of her old friend. 'Roger himself is so magnificent,' she wrote to Vanessa, 'I'm so in love with him'. Early versions were sent to Helen Anrep (Roger's partner for the last eight years of his life) and his sister Margery for corrections. Virginia felt a sense of 'constraint', of 'other people looking over one's shoulder' and took to her bed. Numerous revisions followed that were hampered by the discovery of new material: 'Its like making a dress thats always having a new arm or leg let in in the skirt.' 'What a grind it is;' she moaned in a diary entry of 26th April 1939, '& I suppose of little interest except to six or seven people. And I shall be abused.' And to Vita in September 1939 she lamented: 'I wrote ten sentences of Roger, but each word was like carrying a coal scuttle to the top of the house.'

The first draft was complete in March 1940, but Leonard 'gave [her] a very severe lecture' on it, stating that she had selected 'the wrong method'. Usually such criticism would have knocked her confidence and precipitated depression, but this time, though she felt as though she was 'being pecked by a very hard strong beak', she had an 'odd gleam, that he was himself on the wrong tack'. However, Leonard did have a point, the book is certainly evasive; it allows Roger's writing too often to stand unanalysed and avoids detailed discussion of his painting (though there was an appendix added about his paintings by Duncan and Vanessa). Nevertheless, both Helen Anrep and Vanessa were pleased. Vanessa wrote to Virginia after reading it in its typescript form in March 1940: 'Since Julian died I haven't been able to think of Roger – now you have brought him back to me. Although I cannot help crying, I can't thank you enough.'[40]

Though the first draft of Roger's biography brought his image back, Vanessa was preoccupied with trying to disentangle her daughter Angelica from her liaison with David Garnett, who was not only over twenty-five years Angelica's senior, but had been her father's lover and had unsuccessfully tried to seduce her mother. The affair was kept secret from Virginia for several years while Vanessa tried to separate the lovers. It was 'a state of things' that made Vanessa 'worried and unhappy' and in April 1940 she warned Garnett to keep his opinions of her relationship with Angelica to himself and pleaded with him to 'realise that before you come to any decision which will affect Angelica's whole life it would be very cruel not to take into account our views in so far as they seem reasonable'. Only the painting of Berwick Church (which still bears the frescos painted by Vanessa and Duncan) seemed to cheer her. When Vanessa finally told Virginia about the affair in May 1940, she reported back to her daughter: 'I don't think V. was as much upset as I had expected. She wasn't exactly pleased!' Virginia, unlike Vanessa, realised that it was pointless to try and stand in Angelica's way publicly, though privately she wrote: 'Pray God she may tire of that rusty surly slow old dog with his amorous ways & his primitive mind.' Though the intimacy of their relationship cooled a little (there was 'not the old family ease'), Virginia still invited Angelica, who had moved with Garnett into a cottage near Charleston and Monk's House, for tea and demanded the usual show of affection from her niece.

From April 1940, following Vanessa's revelations and the typescript draft of *Roger Fry*, the war began to edge closer, both physically and intellectually. Virginia tried to make a stand against its insidious presence in literature to the Workers' Educational Association at Brighton (the lecture was published by the Hogarth Press as *The Leaning Tower* on 27th April 1940). In this lecture Virginia suggested that politics had distorted and deformed the poetry of the younger generation, arguing that: 'It explains the pedagogic, the didactic, the loud-speaker strain that dominates their poetry.' Shortly after this lecture, on 13th May 1940, Winston Churchill took over from Chamberlain to form a national coalition government and it was his voice who now dominated the airwaves in every major crisis of the war ('Churchill exhorting all men to stand together'; 'Churchill asked us to reflect'; 'The Government is not capitulating. Churchill to broadcast'; 'A clear, measured, robust speech'). In June, while writing her memoirs, she was contemplating the German invasion and discussed suicide with friends should the worst happen: 'If we are beaten then – however we solve that problem, and one solution is apparently suicide (so it was decided three nights ago in London among us) – book writing becomes doubtful. But I wish to go on, not to settle down in that dismal puddle.' She began to carry morphia, prescribed by her brother Adrian, in her pocket, but recorded in various diary entries her desire to keep on living, though she imagined how death might feel: 'painful? Yes. Terrifying. I suppose so – Then a swoon; a drum; two or three gulps attempting consciousness – & then, dot dot dot'. On 11th June 1940, Mussolini joined in on Hitler's side. She papered her windows; dissuaded Leonard from joining the Local Defence Volunteers (which became the Home Guard); and attended talks in the village hall on 'how charcoal absorbs gas' and how to climb out of a window safely. After these lessons she confided to her diary: 'I dont like any of the feelings war breeds: patriotism; communal &c, all sentimental & emotional parodies of our real feelings. But then, we're in for it. Every day we have our raids: at night the bloodhounds are out.' She felt that they were 'pour[ing] to the edge of a precipice'. Friends became more important, her correspondence with Vita was more frequent and loving than it had been in the 1930s and, while the Germans invaded Paris, she spent a lazy day at Penshurst with Leonard, Vita and Gwen St Aubyn on 14th June 1940. 'Odd to have seen this Elizabethan great house the first day that invasion becomes serious,' she reflected.

Roger Fry was published on 25th July 1940 in the face of these thoughts and fears, a few days after the French surrender and just over a month before the London Blitz began in earnest. Reviews were largely good, Desmond MacCarthy's in *The Sunday Times* was glowing:

> Desmond's review really says all I wanted said. The book delights friends & the younger generation say Yes, yes we know him; & its not only delightful but important. Thats enough. And it gave me a very calm rewarded feeling – not the old triumph, as over a novel; but the feeling I've done what was asked of me, given my friends what they wanted.

Herbert Read in *The Spectator* liked it, but disliked Fry ('polite to me; very mean & spiteful about R.'), while Forster in the *New Statesman & Nation* thought it had a higher purpose and read it as 'a noble and convincing defence of civilisation'.[41] The book sold well and they were soon printing a third time, much to Virginia's surprise. Her friends were congratulatory; Desmond, Clive, Ethel, Ruth Fry (Roger's youngest sister) wrote to say they liked it. Bessie Trevelyan compared it to music, which evoked a detailed response from Virginia who replied: 'You have found out exactly what I was trying to do when you compare it to a piece of music. Its odd, for I'm not regularly musical, but I always think of my books as music before I write them.' She confided to Bessie that 'nobody – none of my friends – made such a difference to my life as he did'. However, Benedict

Nicolson elicited the most interesting responses from Virginia when he criticized Roger, and Bloomsbury more generally, for not doing more to stop Nazism. The letters she sent to Ben contained a spirited and well-reasoned defence listing and then deconstructing all of his arguments, particularly those surrounding his criticism that Roger and Bloomsbury were elitist and cut off from the rest of humanity (it is a criticism still levelled at the Bloomsbury Group today and her response is therefore worth quoting at length):

'My quarrel' you say 'is not with art but with Bloomsbury.' What do you mean by Bloomsbury? It is rather as if I should say, My quarrel is not with art but with Mayfair, meaning by Mayfair Ben Nicolson, Vita, Eddie Sackville, the Sitwells, Stephen Tennant and David Cecil. You would feel I meant something vaguely abusive, but you would find it very difficult to say what. Apparently you mean by 'Bloomsbury' a set of people who sat on the floor at Bernard Street saying 'More and more I understand nothing of humanity in the mass' and were content with that, instead of trying to make humanity in the mass understand and appreciate what you know and say. It was Roger Fry who said 'I understand nothing of humanity in the mass.' I did not say that: if you impute that to me, then you must also impute to me his saying 'More and more I dread the imprisonment of egotism.' You must make me responsible for teaching elementary school children in the black country how to dress, for setting up the Omega, for decorating the walls of the Boro Polytechnic.

But in fact I am not responsible for anything Roger did or said. My own education and my own point of view were entirely different from his. [...] When I was a young woman I tried to share the fruits of [my] very imperfect education with the working classes by teaching literature at Morley College; by holding a Womens Cooperative

Guild meeting weekly; and, politically, by working for the vote. It is true I wrote books and some of those books [...] have sold many thousand copies. That is, I did my best to make them reach a far wider circle than a little private circle of exquisite and cultivated people. And to some extent I succeeded. Leonard too is Bloomsbury. He has spent half his life in writing books like International Government, like the Barbarians at the gates, like Empire and Commerce, to prevent the growth of Nazism; and to create a League of Nations. Maynard Keynes is Bloomsbury. He wrote the [*Economic*] Consequences of the Peace. Lytton Strachey was Bloomsbury. His books had a very large circulation and certainly influenced a wider circle than any small group. Duncan has made a living ever since he was a boy by painting. These are facts about Bloomsbury and they do seem to me to prove that they have done their very best to make humanity in the mass appreciate what they knew and saw.

She concluded pointedly: 'I cant find your answer in your letter, how it is that you are going to change the attitudes of the mass of people by remaining an art critic.' Benedict was not alone in his criticism of the coterie atmosphere of Bloomsbury, but it was to him she made one of her most coherent and convincing defences.

In July, as *Roger Fry* came out, the Battle of Britain began with raids on the Channel fleet, but this soon became an attack on the coastal airfields and much of the aerial battle in August 1940 was fought in the hot summer skies above Monk's House. The Woolfs lay flat under the trees in their back garden relieved that they would be 'broken together', and listened to the 'pop, pop, pop' of the machine guns and the roar of engines while playing bowls on the terrace. In London, they moved from Tavistock Square to Mecklenburg Square, but the house there was damaged and then made uninhabitable by a time-bomb in November, while Tavistock had been completely destroyed the month before. Leonard and John Lehmann decided to move the press to the Garden City Press at Letchworth, which would prove to be a smart move as the Hogarth Press did not lose as much stock as other London publishers did in the Blitz. The Woolfs decamped to Rodmell taking as many of their possessions with them as possible, though living among the boxes made Virginia wish that Hitler had obliterated it all. They took solace in gardening, cooking and playing bowls, but even in rural isolation, there were bomb scares; one burst the banks of the Ouse and the valley became a lake, much to Virginia's delight, though she did fall into the floodwater in November 1940. However, she was much more afraid of the invasion of 'd–d Anreps' that Vanessa had seemingly orchestrated by telling Helen Anrep that there was a cottage free in Virginia's village.

Throughout these years, Virginia was working on two projects as relief from *Roger Fry*: a novel, provisionally entitled 'Pointz Hall', and her autobiography. She was always suggesting to family and friends, including Violet Dickinson, Lady Ottoline Morrell and Lady Robert Cecil, that they should write their memoirs; she enthused about the ones who did (she was particularly excited about Bertrand Russell's and Ethel's) and championed the memoirs of Elizabeth Robins, which she recommended to her American publishers, Harcourt Brace, in August 1939. 'Letters and memoirs are my delight – how much better than novels!' Virginia exclaimed to Violet and later confessed, 'I'm so old I could write a life of myself. But I remember too much.' She had begun making notes for her memoirs in 1939; she had already written several papers for The Memoir Club; and she had also given an amusing talk on the Dreadnought Hoax for the Women's Institute in July 1940. Her diary was half written as future material for them: 'this will make interesting reading to me one of these days, should I write a true memoir'; and she thought that 'one day I may brew a tiny ingot out of it'. She began writing about her childhood and noted in her diary in April 1940: 'My mother, I was thinking had 2 characters. I was thinking of my memoirs. The platform of time. How I see father from the 2 angles. As a child condemning; as a woman of 58 understanding – I shd say tolerating. Both views true?' In writing about her father, whom she loved and disliked, she interestingly imbued him at this time with some of the traits she despised in the European dictators, such as masculine egotism and dramatic histrionics. In October she 'unwound a page about Thoby' and in November she was describing the period between Stella's and her father's deaths. The fragment of her memoir that she wrote in the 1940s can be found in *Moments of Being* as 'A Sketch of the Past'.

The beginnings of *Between the Acts* (1941), on the other hand, can be traced back as far as January 1933 when she perceived 'the shape of pure poetry beckoning me' while she was writing *The Years*. After the completion of *The Years* she wondered: 'Will another novel ever swim up? If so, how? The only hint I have towards it is that its to be dialogue: & poetry: & prose; all quite distinct. No more long, closely written books.' However, Virginia only began imagining the novel properly on 12th April 1938: 'Last night I began making up again: Summers night: a complete whole: that's my idea.' Later that month, in greater detail, she scribbled:

why not Poyntzet Hall: a centre: all lit. discussed in connection with real little incongruous living humour; & anything that comes into my head; but 'I' rejected: 'We' substituted: to whom at the end there shall be an invocation? 'We'… composed of many different things… we all life, all art, all waifs & strays – a rambling capricious but somehow unified whole – the present state of my mind? And English country; & a scenic old house – & a terrace where nursemaids walk? & people passing – & a perpetual variety & change from intensity to prose. & facts – & notes; & – but eno'.

The idea of the continuum of history in which we all play a minor role as part of humanity was influenced, though not inspired, by her meeting with Freud in January 1939 (at which he gave her a narcissus). After this meeting she began to read his works for the first time, though she had mixed feelings about his sense of humans as having a collective instinct: 'Freud is upsetting: reducing one to a whirlpool'. She was interested in his ideas on prehistory and group consciousness and the concept that we are all 'orts, scraps and fragments', a refrain from Shakespeare's *Troilus and Cressida* that is repeated several times in the novel. *Between the Acts* is set on a summer's day just before the Second World War in a village where the locals are putting on a pageant of English history for the gentry at Pointz Hall; the pageant allowed her to address this idea of the collective 'we'. The style of the novel is similarly interesting for it tells the story of the relationships between the characters on this summer's day in a mixture of drama, poetry and prose, just as her 1927 essay 'Poetry, Fiction and the Future' had predicted.

Drama was integral to the story and the style of the novel; even the title uses the image of theatre to describe the sense of waiting between the First and Second World Wars. Leonard Woolf was also writing his political play *The Hotel* over the period of the novel's inception and their attempts to have it staged are catalogued in a number of letters. However, unlike Leonard's *The Hotel*, *Between the Acts* used the political climate as a backdrop rather than as a plot and made no attempt to comment (at least openly) on the lead up to war and the major political figures. Virginia was also increasingly involved with the village players in Rodmell who partly inspired the idea for the pageant (along with E.M. Forster's pageants of the 1930s). 'We're acting village plays; written by the gardener's wife, and the chauffeur's wife; and acted by the other villagers,' Virginia noted in a 1940 letter to her niece Ann Stephen. Virginia had also been asked to write a play for the Rodmell Women's Institute and, in a letter to Margaret Llewelyn Davies, described the climate of village life in which the piece would be performed: 'I'm becoming, you'll be amused to hear, an active member of the Womens Institute, who've just asked me to write a play for the villagers to act. And to produce it myself. I should like to if I could.' Sadly, this play did not materialise other than as the pageant performed by the villagers of her final novel.

The Woolfs' voluntary exile to Rodmell due to the war assisted in the representation of village life in the novel as they became increasingly embroiled in the 'doings' of the villagers. 'Oh dear,' she lamented to Margaret Llewelyn Davies, 'how full of doings villages are – and of violent quarrels and of incessant intrigues. The hatred for the parsons wife passes belief. We're thought red hot revolutionaries because the Labour party meets in our dining room.' She used her servant Louie Everest's brother who had mental health problems as inspiration for the village idiot and also drew on the villagers' stoicism as they sat through a village play ignoring the air-raid siren: 'We had a fête: also a village play. The sirens sounded in the middle. All the mothers sat stolid. I also admired that very much.' Such scenes are translated into *Between the Acts* as subtle reminders of the conflict in Europe, thus contributing to the novel's feeling of foreboding.

However, as the war progressed Virginia's writing seemed to her to be increasingly pointless as her sense of having an audience disappeared. In a diary entry of 9th June 1940, Virginia recorded that 'the writing "I", has vanished. No audience. No echo. Thats part of one's death' and later that year in a letter to Ethel dated 11th September 1940, she reiterated this sense of loss: 'Its odd to feel one's writing in a vacuum – no-one will read it. I feel the audience has gone. Still, so oddly is one made, I find I must spin my brain even in a vacuum'. She finished the first draft in November 1940 and the final version on 25th February 1941. Upon completion, she described her novel as 'the Pageant: the Play – finally Between the Acts'.

Throughout the final drafting of *Between the Acts* the bombs fell on 'majestic' London and the English countryside around

Rodmell, and Virginia became more and more depressed. She wrote 'Thoughts on Peace in an Air Raid' for *The New Republic* which came out on 21st October 1940, while her shorter fiction became darker, laced with symbols of foreboding such as 'The Legacy', 'The Symbol' and 'The Searchlight', all published post-humously. Vanessa wrote of the latter: 'It seems to me lovely, only too full of suggestions for pictures almost. They leap into my mind at every turn. Your writing always does that for me to some extent, but I think this one more than usual.'[42] Virginia continued to mould her memories, but the pressure of confronting her past combined with the freezing winter and the war led her to give up her memoir writing in January 1941. She was also working on a critical book meant to give a history of English literature, which she had provisionally entitled 'Reading at Random' or 'Turning the Page'. The idea for it had surfaced in a diary entry dated as early as 14th February 1934 and she had been considering its style in June 1940: 'I wish I cd invent a new critical method – something swifter & lighter & more colloquial & yet intense: more to the point & less composed; more fluid & following the flight, than in my C.R. essays.' However, she did not start drafting the first two chapters, entitled 'Anon' and 'The Reader', until February and March 1941. On 1st March 1941 she wrote to Ethel Smyth: 'I am at the moment trying, without the least success, to write an article or two for a new Common Reader', but less than two weeks later in a letter to Elizabeth Robins she confessed that the war was rendering her writing both impossible and pointless by taking away both her audience and her inspiration: 'Its difficult, I find, to write. No audience. No private stimulus, only this outer roar.' She became very thin and weak; Leonard consulted Dr Octavia Wilberforce.

In March 1941 it became increasingly apparent to Leonard and Octavia that Virginia's mental state was becoming desperate. On 18th March she came home to Monk's House drenched, having fallen into a dyke. Leonard suggested in his autobiography that this was a failed suicide attempt and he recalls having 'an automatic feeling of desperate uneasiness'.[43] It is thought that she wrote the first of her three suicide letters on this day. Leonard warned Vanessa that a crisis was impending and Vanessa came to tea, after which she wrote to Virginia: 'You *must* be sensible, which means you must accept the fact that Leonard and I can judge better than you can. [...] what should I have done all these last 3 years if you hadn't been able to keep me alive and cheerful. You don't know how much I depend on you.'[44] On 27th March 1941, Virginia wrote to John Lehmann asking him not to publish *Between the Acts*, it was 'too silly and trivial' she said and needed revising. Leonard posted the letter with one from himself explaining Virginia's precarious mental state and suggesting that publication should be put off until the autumn. He arranged a professional meeting for Virginia with Octavia on 27th March in Brighton where Virginia spoke about her fears, insecurities, her past and her body.

Virginia drafted two more suicide letters: one to Vanessa which was most likely written on 23rd March and one to Leonard thought to have been written on 28th March, though it was the earlier one for Leonard arguably written on the 18th that she left for him along with Vanessa's when she left Monk's House on 28th March 1941. Virginia went for a walk along the River Ouse; she stopped on the bank to pick up a stone and put it in her pocket and then walked into the river. When Leonard saw the letters he went to look for her, but only found her walking stick and footprints by the water's edge. The police were called and the river was dragged, but Virginia's body was not found. Vanessa wrote to Vita as 'the person Virginia loved most I think outside her own family' on 29th March 1941 to warn her that Virginia was missing, presumed dead.[45] Over the next few days Leonard tried to keep busy, while Vanessa was resigned and stoic. She wrote to Vita on 2nd April:

Leonard is working hard, going to London to committees, etc. I think he'll simply plunge into work. He told me if he had it all over again he would do the same, and so I suppose he realises he's not to blame actually. In fact I think nothing could have prevented the possibility just then – only I wish I had realised it, but I didn't at all. Even the last time when she talked to me about herself, that possibility never occurred to me. How strange it seems.[46]

Vanessa felt that the loss of her sister, one of the linchpins of their society, meant the end of 'family weekly meetings': 'They would be so pointless without her,' she said.[47]

Virginia's body was eventually found a little way downstream on 18th April by children on a picnic. An inquest was held and the verdict returned was 'suicide while the balance of her mind was disturbed'. The cremation took place on 21st April with only Leonard present; after which he took her ashes back to Monk's House where they were buried, without a ceremony, under the elm tree that they had named Virginia (the other large elm was Leonard). As Vanessa said to Vita, 'anything else would have been too uncharacteristic',[48] and she recalled how Leonard broke down in tears when he told Vanessa how he wished Virginia to be buried, worrying that she might think him sentimental. A simple plaque was placed over her ashes bearing the penultimate sentence of The Waves: 'Against you I will fling myself, unvanquished and unyielding, O Death!' After the inquest the newspapers announced Virginia's death, and many attributed her suicide to the pressure of the war. Vanessa stated in a letter: 'Of course all the reporters got the letters wrong. Virginia really said something like "I feel I am going mad again and I can't face those terrible times again." Nothing about "these terrible times." It sounded so unlike her.'[49] Leonard then had to defend her memory against attack from the Bishop of Lincoln's wife who claimed in The Sunday Times Virginia had no right to give up on the war effort. Both Leonard and Desmond MacCarthy responded clearly, but firmly that Virginia had always suffered from mental illness and her suicide was caused by her fear of madness, not her fear of the Nazis. Poor Leonard also received an anonymous letter saying 'The coroner has been very kind to you', which as Vanessa stated to Vita was 'incredible'.[50] In a recollection of Virginia, Rosamond Lehmann was clear, as were all those who knew Virginia, in her defence: 'It is important to say this in view of the distasteful myths which have risen around her death: the conception of her as a morbid individual, one who "couldn't face life", and put an end to it out of hysterical self-pity. No. She lived under the shadow of the fear of madness; but her sanity was exquisite'.[51]

Following Virginia's death Leonard became her literary executor. He ignored her command to destroy all her papers, and he and Lehmann slowly and systematically began to release her unpublished material. *Between the Acts* was published on 17th July 1941 to mixed reviews. David Cecil argued in the *Spectator* on 18th July that the novel looks at 'the essential truth about life', its 'beauty' and 'mutability',[52] but criticized the style, which for him, as a fusion of realism and poetry, did not succeed. 'It must be counted as in part a failure,' he wrote.[53] The *TLS* review on 19th July called it 'a rarefied touching and imperfect book'.[54] 'On the one side of experience is perpetuity, continuity, timeless and changeless order; on the other the bright evanescent bubble of human mutability.'[55] Many reviewers took the opportunity to dwell on her oeuvre as a whole because of her death, one or two, such as Frank Swinnerton in *The Observer*, leapt at the chance to have one last dig: 'She was like somebody bedridden in a house in the country, hearing and explaining every sound [...] although her intellect was not powerful it had grace and distinction.'[56]

In recollections of Virginia, family and friends returned to three central themes: her beauty, her humour and her imagination. All of them resisted the idea of her as an invalid aesthete. Virginia's brother-in-law, Clive Bell, recalled the effect that her combination of humour and imagination would have on a visit: '[it] would be exciting, we knew that we were going to laugh and be surprised and made to feel that the temperature of life was several degrees higher than we had supposed', but he also cautioned that this meant 'she saw life and to some extent experienced it as a novel or rather as a series of novels, in which anyone of her friends might find him or herself cast, all unawares, for a part.'[57] He warned 'the reader who itches to compose histories or biographies, that the author's accounts of people and of their sayings and doings may be flights of her airy imagination'.[58] Leonard Woolf described this process more clearly:

> She would be describing what she had seen in the street, for instance, or what someone had said to her, and then go on to weave a character of the person and everything connected with them, and it would be quite amusing. Then suddenly it would become something entirely different. I always called it leaving the ground. She would weave not the sort of scene or conversation which one felt was what anyone else would have seen and described, but something entirely different. It was often extraordinarily amusing, but in a very peculiar way – almost like a fantasy, and sometimes it was extremely beautiful.[59]

Many friends recalled the quality of her conversation. Frances Marshall called it 'dazzling'; Rose Macaulay saw it as 'a stimulating entertainment'; Gerald Brenan remembered 'conversation of a brilliance and [...] spontaneity which, I imagine, has rarely been heard in England before'.[60] Barbara Bagenal recalled that her company was sought by children as well as adults: 'Vanessa asked the children whom, of all their friends and relations, they particularly wanted to invite. They all shouted at once "Virginia!"'[61] Like the children, Clive Bell and Lytton Strachey both decided that she was always the person they would most like to see:

> I remember spending some dark, uneasy, winter days during the first war in the depth of the country with Lytton Strachey. After lunch, as we watched the rain pour down and premature darkness roll up, he said, in his searching,

personal way, 'Loves apart, whom would you most like to see coming up the drive?' I hesitated a moment and he supplied the answer: 'Virginia, of course.'[62]

Nevertheless, the legend of the invalid genius was, and still is, dominant in the press, in spite of evidence to the contrary to be found in her diaries, letters and memoirs, and in the recollections of family and friends. Elizabeth Bowen claimed to 'get a curious shock when [she saw] people regarding her entirely as a martyred... or definitely tragic sort of person, claimed by the darkness'; E.M. Forster asked that the public 'dismiss the legend of the Invalid Lady of Bloomsbury', while Clive Bell described it as 'a silly caricature'.[63]

'I must not settle into a figure,' Virginia had written in March 1932; it was a worry that in many ways has come to pass. Nicole Kidman's portrayal of Virginia in Stephen Daldry's film of Michael Cunningham's *The Hours*, and the wide selection of merchandise bearing her image (from shopping bags to mouse-mats, from tea towels to mugs), suggest that she has indeed settled into a figure. The scholarship surrounding Virginia and her writing is overwhelming; there is an International Virginia Woolf Society; an annual conference and an annual journal; a miscellany and a bulletin dedicated to her life and work; and there are lengthy biographies by Hermione Lee, James King and her nephew Quentin Bell among others. The majority of her papers are split between the Monk's House Collection at Sussex University and the Berg Collection in the New York Public Library. Novels, films and plays about her life and work are regularly advertised. Just as Virginia delighted in fictionalising other people, so the public has delighted in mythologising her. Though her image and personality have been distorted over time, there are few who could argue against her reputation as one of the greatest diarists, correspondents and fiction writers of the early twentieth century. She was, as her family and friends often agreed, something of a genius.

Notes

1. Joan Russell Noble (ed.), *Recollections of Virginia Woolf*, London: PeterOwen, 1972, p. 13.

2. Letters from Vanessa Bell to Virginia Stephen dated 4th May 1927 and 14th October 1938 (The Berg Collection).

3. Letter from Vanessa Bell to Virginia Stephen dated 31st October 1904 (The Berg Collection).

4. Letter from Vanessa Bell to Clive Bell dated Sunday probably September 1910 (Charleston Papers, Tate Britain).

5. Angelica Garnett in Joan Russell Noble (ed.), *Recollections of Virginia Woolf*, London: Peter Owen, 1972, p. 84.

6. Virginia Woolf, 'Introduction' to *Victorian Photographs of Famous Men & Fair Women*, London: The Hogarth Press, 1973, p. 14.

7. Vanessa Bell, 'Notes on Virginia's Childhood' in J.H. Stape (ed.), *Virginia Woolf: Interviews and Recollections*, London: Macmillan, 1995, p. 5.

8. Ibid. p. 3.

9. Letter from Leslie Stephen to Julia Stephen dated 25 January 1887, Berg Collection.

10. Vanessa Bell, 'Notes on Virginia's Childhood' in J.H. Stape (ed.), *Virginia Woolf: Interviews and Recollections*, London: Macmillan, 1995, p. 7.

11. Letters from Leslie Stephen to Julia Stephen dated 29th July 1893 and 3rd August 1893, Berg Collection.

12. Vanessa Bell, 'Notes on Virginia's Childhood' in J.H. Stape (ed.), *Virginia Woolf: Interviews and Recollections*, London: Macmillan, 1995, p. 3.

13. Joan Russell Noble (ed.) *Recollections of Virginia Woolf*, London: Peter Owen, 1972, p. 20.

14. Leonard Woolf, *Beginning Again: An Autobiography of the Years 1911–1918*, London: Hogarth Press, 1964, p. 21.

15. Quentin Bell, *Virginia Woolf: A Biography*, Vol. 1, London: Hogarth Press, 1972, p. 133.

16. Virginia Woolf, *The Platform of Time*, S.P. Rosenbaum (ed.), London: Hesperus, 2008, p. 197.

17. Frances Spalding, *Vanessa Bell*, London: Weidenfeld & Nicolson, 1983, p. 92.

18. Leonard Woolf, *Sowing: An Autobiography of the Years 1880–1904*, London: The Hogarth Press, 1964, p. 184.

19. Leonard Woolf, *Beginning Again: An Autobiography of the Years 1911–1918*, London: Hogarth Press, 1964, p. 69.

20. Robin Majumdar and Allen McLaurin (eds.), *Virginia Woolf: The Critical Heritage*, London: Routledge and Kegan Paul, 1975, p. 64.
21. G.E. Easdale in J.H. Stape, (ed.) *Virginia Woolf: Interviews and Recollections*, London: Macmillan, 1995, p. 18.
22. Robin Majumdar and Allen McLaurin (eds.), *Virginia Woolf: The Critical Heritage*, London: Routledge and Kegan Paul, 1975, p. 82.
23. Ibid. p. 108.
24. Ibid. p. 107–8.
25. Ibid. p. 113.
26. William Pryor (ed.), *Virginia Woolf and the Raverats: A Different Sort of Friendship*, Bath: Clear Books, 2003, p. 153.
27. Vita Sackville-West, *The Letters of Vita Sackville-West to Virginia Woolf*, Louise DeSalvo and Mitchell A. Leaska (eds.), London: Macmillan, 1985, p. 252.
28. Ibid. p. 306.
29. Robin Majumdar and Allen McLaurin (eds.), *Virginia Woolf: The Critical Heritage*, London: Routledge and Kegan Paul, p. 236.
30. *The Daily Chronicle*, November 1928 quoted in Victoria Glendinning, Vita, London: Weidenfeld and Nicolson, 1983, p. 205.
31. Unpublished letter from Virginia Woolf to Mr Davis n.p.n.d, Berg Collection.
32. Robin Majumdar and Allen McLaurin (eds.), *Virginia Woolf: The Critical Heritage*, London: Routledge and Kegan Paul, p. 259.
33. Ibid. p. 271.
34. Quentin Bell, *Virginia Woolf: A Biography*, Vol. 2, London: Hogarth Press, 1972, p. 189.
35. Vanessa Bell, *Selected Letters of Vanessa Bell,* Regina Marler (ed.), London: Bloomsbury, 1993, p. 424.
36. Ibid. p. 423.
37. Ibid. p. 428.
38. Ibid. p. 475.
39. Robin Majumdar and Allen McLaurin (eds.), *Virginia Woolf: The Critical Heritage*, London: Routledge and Kegan Paul, p. 410.
40. Vanessa Bell, *Selected Letters of Vanessa Bell,* Regina Marler (ed.), London: Bloomsbury, 1993, p. 461.
41. Robin Majumdar and Allen McLaurin (eds.), *Virginia Woolf: The Critical Heritage*, London: Routledge and Kegan Paul, p. 425.
42. Vanessa Bell, *Selected Letters of Vanessa Bell,* Regina Marler (ed.), London: Bloomsbury, 1993, p. 454.
43. Leonard Woolf, *The Journey Not the Arrival Matters: An Autobiography of the Years 1939–1969*, London: The Hogarth Press, 1964, p. 91.
44. Vanessa Bell, *Selected Letters of Vanessa Bell,* Regina Marler (ed.), London: Bloomsbury, 1993, p. 474.

45. Ibid.

46. Ibid. p. 475.

47. Ibid. p. 476.

48. Ibid.

49. Ibid. p. 479.

50. Ibid.

51. In Joan Russell Noble (ed.), *Recollections of Virginia Woolf*, London: Peter Owen, 1972, p. 63.

52. Robin Majumdar and Allen McLaurin (eds.), *Virginia Woolf: The Critical Heritage*, London: Routledge and Kegan Paul, p. 436.

53. Ibid. p. 437.

54. Ibid. p. 439.

55. Ibid. p. 440.

56. Ibid. p. 442.

57. In Joan Russell Noble (ed.), *Recollections of Virginia Woolf*, London: Peter Owen, 1972, p. 73 and p. 70.

58. Ibid. p. 69.

59. In J.H. Stape (ed.), *Virginia Woolf: Interviews and Recollections*, London: Macmillan, 1995, p. 147.

60. In Joan Russell Noble (ed.), *Recollections of Virginia Woolf*, London: Peter Owen, 1972, p. 75 and p. 164 and J.H. Stape (ed.), *Virginia Woolf: Interviews and Recollections*, London: Macmillan, 1995, p. 90.

61. In Joan Russell Noble (ed.), *Recollections of Virginia Woolf*, London: Peter Owen, 1972, p. 153.

62. Clive Bell quoted in S.P. Rosenbaum (ed.), *The Bloomsbury Group: A collection of memoirs and commentary*, University of Toronto Press, 1995, p. 98.

63. In Joan Russell Noble (ed.), *Recollections of Virginia Woolf*, London: Peter Owen, 1972, p. 50 and p. 185 and J.H. Stape (ed.), *Virginia Woolf: Interviews and Recollections*, London: Macmillan, 1995, p. 98.

Bibliography

Considering the plethora of scholarship surrounding Virginia Woolf's life and work, this bibliography is necessarily selective. There are many more biographies than are listed here, so only the most influential have been included. For the novels I have used and suggested the Oxford World's Classics editions, but any good recent edition by Penguin or Norton would be equally suitable. The new Cambridge scholarly edition of Woolf's novels would also be of interest to the more advanced reader of her work.

Bell, Quentin. *Virginia Woolf: A Biography*, Vols 1 and 2, London: Hogarth Press, 1972.

Bell, Vanessa. *Selected Letters of Vanessa Bell*, Regina Marler (ed.), London: Bloomsbury, 1993.

Cameron, Julia Margaret. *Victorian Photographs of Famous Men & Fair Women*, London: Hogarth Press, 1973.

Garnett, Angelica. *Deceived with Kindness*, London: Pimlico, 1995.

Glendinning, Victoria. *Vita*, London: Weidenfeld and Nicolson, 1983.

Hussey, Mark. *Virginia Woolf A to Z: A Comprehensive Reference for Students, Teachers, and Common Readers to Her Life, Work and Critical Reception*, New York: Facts on File, 1995.

Kennedy, Richard. *A Boy at the Hogarth Press*, London: Hesperus Press, 2011.

King, James. *Virginia Woolf*, London: Penguin, 1994.

Lee, Hermione. *Virginia Woolf*, London: Vintage, 1997.

Noble, Joan Russell (ed.). *Recollections of Virginia Woolf*, London: Peter Owen, 1972.

Majumdar, Robin and McLaurin, Allen (eds.). *Virginia Woolf: The Critical Heritage*, London: Routledge and Kegan Paul, 1975.

Raitt, Suzanne. *Vita and Virginia: The Work and Friendship of V. Sackville-West and Virginia Woolf*, Oxford: Oxford University Press, 1993.

Sackville-West, Vita. *The Letters of Vita Sackville-West to Virginia Woolf*, Louise DeSalvo and Mitchell A. Leaska (eds.), London: Macmillan, 1985.

Sellers, Susan. *The Cambridge Companion to Virginia Woolf*, Cambridge University Press, 2010.

Shone, Richard. *Bloomsbury Portraits: Vanessa Bell, Duncan Grant and their Circle*, Oxford: Phaidon, 1976.

Silver, Brenda R. *Virginia Woolf's Reading Notebooks*, Princeton University Press, 1983.

Spalding, Frances. *Vanessa Bell*, London: Weidenfeld & Nicolson, 1983.

Stape, J.H. (ed.). *Virginia Woolf: Interviews and Recollections*, London: Macmillan, 1995.

Stephen, Sir Leslie. *The Mausoleum Book*, Oxford: Clarendon Press, 1977.

Woolf, Leonard. *Sowing: An Autobiography of the Years 1880–1904*, London: Hogarth Press, 1967.

———. *Growing: An Autobiography of the Years 1904–1911*, London: Hogarth Press, 1961.

———. *Beginning Again: An Autobiography of the Years 1911–1918*, London: Hogarth Press, 1964.

———. *Downhill All the Way: An Autobiography of the Years 1919–1939*, London: Hogarth Press, 1967.

———. *The Journey Not the Arrival Matters: An Autobiography of the Years 1939–1969*, London: Hogarth Press, 1969.

Woolf, Virginia. *Between the Acts*, Oxford University Press, 2008 (1941).

———. *Collected Essays*, 4 vols, New York: Harcourt, Brace & World, 1967.

———. *The Common Reader*, London: Vintage, 2003 (1925).

———. *The Common Reader, Second Series*, London: Vintage, 2003 (1932).

_____. *The Diary of Virginia Woolf*, 5 vols, Anne Olivier Bell (ed.), London: Hogarth Press, 1977–1984.

_____. *Flush: A Biography*, London: Penguin, 1983 (1933).

_____. *Freshwater*, Lucio Ruotolo (ed.), New York: Harcourt Brace Jovanovich, 1976.

_____. *Jacob's Room*, Oxford University Press, 1992 (1922).

_____. *The Letters of Virginia Woolf*, Nigel Nicolson and Joanne Trautmann (eds.), 6 vols, London: Hogarth Press, 1975–1980.

_____. *Mrs Dalloway*, Oxford University Press, 2009 (1925).

_____. *Moments of Being*, Jeanne Schulkind (ed.), San Diego: Harvest/Harcourt Brace Jovanovich, 1985.

_____. *Night and Day*, Oxford University Press, 1999 (1920).

_____. *Orlando: A Biography*, Oxford University Press, 2008 (1928).

_____. *A Passionate Apprentice: The Early Journals – 1897–1909*, Mitchell A. Leaska (ed.), London: Hogarth Press, 1990.

_____. *Roger Fry: A Biography*, London: Hogarth Press, 1991 (1940).

_____. *A Room of One's Own and Three Guineas*, Oxford University Press, 1992 (1929).

_____. *The Complete Shorter Fiction of Virginia Woolf*, Susan Dick (ed.), London: Hogarth Press, 1989.

_____. *To the Lighthouse*, Oxford University Press, 2008 (1927).

_____. *The Voyage Out*, Oxford University Press, 2009 (1915).

_____. *The Waves*, Oxford University Press, 2008 (1931).

_____. *The Years*, Oxford University Press, 2009 (1937).

Archival Sources

The Virginia Woolf Manuscripts from the Henry W. and Albert A. Berg Collection at the New York Public Library, microfilm, 21 reels, Woodbridge, CT: Research Publications International, 1993.

The Virginia Woolf Manuscripts from The Monk's House Papers at the University of Sussex Archive, microfilm, 6 reels, Reading: Primary Source Microfilm; Brighton: Harvester Microform Publications, c.1985.

Permission to quote from unpublished letters of Sir Leslie Stephen and Virginia Woolf kindly granted by The Society of Authors as the Literary Representative of their Estates and The Henry W. and Albert A. Berg Collection of English and American Literature, The New York Public Library Astor, Lenox and Tilden Foundations.

Permission to quote from the unpublished letters of Vanessa Bell kindly granted by her literary executor Henrietta Bell.

Biographical note

Elizabeth Wright is senior lecturer in English at Bath Spa University, where she teaches a module on Virginia Woolf. She has worked as a researcher on the new Cambridge edition of Woolf's novels and has published several articles on Woolf and the Bloomsbury Group. She has also written and produced a dramatic adaptation of Susan Sellers's *Vanessa and Virginia* and is currently writing a book on Woolf and theatre.